"From the moment I began reading *Ignite Your Joy*, I did not want to do anything except keep reading! It's fabulous, I love it. The book is filled with wonderful practical tools and exercises to help you become more joyful, more connected, more calm. These are beautifully woven with Debbie's own personal story of love, loss, and courage. Thank you, Debbie, for writing such a beautiful, practical, and inspirational book."

Lisa Cutler, Executive Women's Coach

"If there is a uniform desire amongst us all, it is the desire to live a life of joy and to invite more love, purpose, and profit into our lives. Debbie Zita's book is filled with practical treasures that will help you to achieve such a life. Interweaving her expertise with her personal experiences and with wisdom from the 'other side,' Debbie's *Ignite Your Joy* provides you with practical and easy to implement suggestions and plans that will help you to truly live a life of joy and abundance. If your soul is yearning for more, then *Ignite your Joy* is a must read."

Ghania Dib, Lawyer and Author

"A great read and learning guide! I encourage women to read this book to get more in touch with yourself in your attempt to 'ignite your joy.' Debbie Zita has quite evidently taken every lesson possible from her own journey and turned it around. She is a woman who radiates the book's true intention. This book is written on a level that keeps it real. If, like most women, you're fighting negative inner voices as you do your best to go through life's journey, it's a must-read for you. Without a doubt, it will be a book I keep flicking back to check in with myself."

Belinda Buchanan, Founder of Hope Child Africa

"Debbie Zita's book will certainly ignite your joy. Her witty and practical way of delivering heart-felt and meaningful words will certainly get you on track to reaching your potential. It is a must-read for every woman seeking more love, purpose, and profit."

Margaret Saunders, Founder of Harmonising Energy Coaching

"I could not put the book down! I love that this book acts like a guide. There are a lot of practical exercises in it that you can implement right now that will change your life. Debbie's personal story is also very inspiring. This is a must-read for anyone embarking on a spiritual journey."

Orsi Parkanyi, Founder and Director of Women as Entrepreneurs

PRAISE FOR *IGNITE YOUR JOY*

"If ever there was a book that made you jump out of bed in the morning with joy for all the world has to offer, this is it. Debbie Zita takes you on a personal and practical journey of learning how to find joy in every moment of our lives. It's the perfect gift for a friend or a loved one; and most importantly, it's one of the best gifts you can give yourself. This book will help you find your purpose and fill your heart with passion so you may experience true, blissful feelings of joy. I enjoyed devouring every delectable, delightful, uplifting page."

Genine Howard, Editor of *Australian Content Magazine*

"Debbie Zita is a person who stands out from the crowd; she speaks up with courage for what she knows and believes in. Her book *Ignite Your Joy,* is a deep exploration utilising her life experience as a intuitive, mother, and fellow traveller to reveal the depth of what real joy is and practical steps on how to ignite it. This is a powerful book for anyone who truly wants to know who they are and to live their full potential. Debbie is a world teacher of global consciousness and her message is recommended reading for those who truly wish to ignite their joy. As you change, your world will change."

Susan Carew, World Peace Clown, Founder of WorldPeacefull

"There are people who just say things to sound authentic and then there are those rare ones whose way of life is a complete expression of their authenticity, which is life changing for those who come in contact with them. Debbie Zita is one such being and this book is a powerful, deeply lived expression of what an authentic woman's way of being truly is. A must-read for every woman seeking her authentic voice."

Mihir Thaker, Executive and Business Coach

"In the true Aussie spirit, Debbie means it when she says she will *Ignite Your Joy*. This book is a no-holds-barred, kick-you-in-the-pants-to-get-you-moving guide to finding what truly brings you joy in your life and becoming a better person in the process. Lots of great exercises and practical advice!"

Daniel Parmeggiani, author of *The Magnificent Truths of Our Existence*

"Debbie Zita has certainly ignited my joy. Her new book is filled with practical and engaging advice to kickstart your pathway back to what inspires and awakens the path to oneself. Read her book and repeat. You'll find your joy awakened here and a fire sparked throughout these carefully crafted pages."

Lawrence Ellyard, CEO and Founder of the International Institute for Complementary Therapists

"I had so much happening in my life, but could literally not peel myself away from Debbie's book. I sat down to read a few pages in between children, work, and renovating, and found myself on page 50 unable to stop reading. Awesome! I am beyond impressed. This is a must-read for people who believe there is more than this reality, who love a bit of magic, and for people who are ready to step into more."

Danielle Tooley, Founder of Vitality and You

"An entertaining read of self-awareness, practical exercises to live a more empowered life, and simply explained spiritual principals that make sense. A must-read for every women who wants to live a more joyous, peaceful, and purposeful life."

Sophie Trpcevski, CEO of The Goal Spot for Women

"*Ignite Your Joy* is a must-read for anyone needing to shift her emotional and spiritual blocks. Debbie is a radiant and fearless woman, and her teachings will fill you with love, passion, and compassion."

Lori Banks, Spiritual Artist and Founder of Illuminated Spirit Art

"Debbie has assisted me in fully claiming all that I am and being proud of it. *Ignite Your Joy* is Debbie's wise and witty expression of the essence of her teachings, which to me have been 'Get out of your own way and let the magic happen!' A must-read for any woman who might be standing in her own way."

Justine McInerney, Singer and Songwriter

"In this beautifully written book, Debbie takes you on a personal and inspirational journey to discover your own unique purpose and uncover your inner joy. This wonderful book combines success principles, motivational insights, and spiritual self-help techniques. A lovely gift for all women wanting to find inner peace and joy."

Michelle Curmi, psychologist and Founder of Mind at Ease and Video Counselling Australia

"This book offers practical encouragement, support, and inspiration for those ready to welcome joy into their lives!"

Fiona Edelstein, Founder of Flavours of Yoga

"Debbie's book offers a spiritual insight into leading a peaceful, satisfying, and most importantly, joyful life. I didn't know that I needed to read it, however, once I started reading, I could not put it down. This is a book everyone should have on their bookshelves."

Aly Walsh, Founder of Aly's Books, author of *When I Left* and *My Mum Says Blah, Blah, Blah*

"Debbie Zita shares her powerful message beautifully. Her wisdom, passion, and practical advice will leave you feeling inspired and ready to inject more joy and purpose into your life. A great book for anyone who's feeling a little flat or disconnected"

Camille Thurnherr, dating and relationship mentor, Founder of Ignite Mr Right

IGNITE
your JOY

How to Invite More Love,
Purpose & Profit into Your Life

Debbie Zita

Unlock Your Best Life Publications
Melbourne, Australia

Copyright (c) 2014 by Debbie Zita. All rights reserved. This book may not be reproduced in whole or in part, stored in a retrieval system, or transmitted in any form or by any means—electronic, mechanical, or other—without written permission from the publisher, except by a reviewer, who may quote brief passages in a review.

Unlock Your Best Life Publications
Website: DebbieZita.com

Editor: Stephanie Gunning
Front cover: Bliss Inventive
Front cover font and interior design:
Fletcher Creative
Cover photo: Amanda Stokes
Hair: Allure Stylists Carnegie
Makeup: Agueda Diaz

978-0-9941646-0-5 (paperback)
978-0-9941646-1-2 (ebook)

1. Self-help 2. Happiness 3. Success
4. Personal finance 5. Spirituality

CONTENTS

Foreword by Luanne Simmons, Chief Goddess, Goddess on Purpose		1
Letter to the Reader		3
Part I	**What's Joy Got to Do with It?**	7
Chapter 1	Why Choose Joy?	9
Chapter 2	Getting Clear on What Brings You Joy	13
Chapter 3	My Joy Story: Mum's the Word	23
Part II	**Love, Loss, and the Cycle of Life**	47
Chapter 4	Choose Love Over Fear	49
Chapter 5	Be Okay with Pissing People Off	65
Chapter 6	Be Your Own Best Friend	71
Chapter 7	Transparent Sisterhood	115
Part III	**Your Life Purpose**	125
Chapter 8	Sing Your Song	127

Chapter 9	Acceptance	151
Part IV	**Your Profit Is Waiting**	171
Chapter 10	What Does Profit Mean to You?	173
Chapter 11	Welcome Conscious Cash	181
Chapter 12	Practical Exercises to Create Abundance	195

Acknowledgments	207
Notes	209
Next Steps	214
Recommended Resources	215
About the Author	223

To my late mother, Eva Sharp, and my late nanna, Ibi Vamos:

Two beautiful angels

FOREWORD
LUANNE SIMMONS

For several years, Debbie Zita and I kept bumping into each other at conferences for women and entrepreneurs in and around Melbourne, Australia, where we were speaking or leading workshops. We'd chat and recognise how likeminded we were, then go our separate ways, always noting that we'd love to get to know each other better, and in the process, gradually becoming friends. I have come to admire Deb's message that women should follow the calling of their souls when designing their lives. She's an example of the archetype I term a *goddess on purpose*. Deb's gifts and insights are magnificent.

In *Ignite Your Joy*, Debbie describes three factors that contribute to a life of great joy and self-discovery: love, purpose, and profit. As her readers, she invites us to examine that in our lives which nourishes our spirit and gives us pleasure, even as it calls forth our brilliance. She guides us to look at the places where we are motivated to serve, and to find ways to sustain ourselves on the path to building a career and lifestyle. She also introduces a model for experiencing abundance on increasingly larger and more inclusive levels of our being that emanate from our connectedness: to ourselves, our families, our friends, our wider community, the world, and the infinite universe. She has a wonderful way of speaking about herself with candor and a pragmatism that grounds the information.

Deb is a remarkable spiritual leader and coach, someone who sees things clearly. My favorite part of her book is when she talks about embracing our Shadow, which is not a place we should be afraid of in any shape or form. The concept of transparent sisterhood is paramount for women everywhere to be supported, nurtured, and mostly heard. It takes feminine leaders like Debbie to gently guide the way for many following in her footsteps.

If you're a woman in transition or choosing to go to the next level in your life, or you're feeling stuck and want to experience more freedom and pleasure, I recommend reading *Ignite Your Joy*.

Luanne Simmons

Chief Goddess, Global Goddess Gatherer, and Divine Business Mentor, Goddess on Purpose

LETTER TO THE READER

Hey there, amazing person.

Yes, I am talking to you. You see, inside each of us is a divine spark of amazingness. Too often we forget to look for that in ourselves and in others. But that doesn't mean it's not there. And when we find our amazingness, every part of our lives changes. We can find work we love to do, our relationships get better, and we make more money.

Part of my joy is helping you (and other women) feel simply amazing about your life and career. It actually makes me feel amazing when I see people recognise their unique amazingness and begin to follow steps of the path it sets out before them.

Welcome to your joy journey. My name is Debbie Zita and I will be your guide for the duration of this book. The reason I say you are on a *journey* is that over the course of researching and writing this book, it became clear to me that JOY actually is a very cool acronym for:

Journey
Of
You

I have been passionate about personal development and spiritual growth since I was young, and actively been immersed in workshops and in creating, learning, and using tools for career success, and most importantly for personal and spiritual transformation, since 1999, my first year out of high school. My primary aim in this book is to share with you the lessons that I've learned along the way about finding work and making money doing the things you love to do that nourish your soul. I also want to provide you with the confidence and knowledge to know that every phase of the journey of your life is beautiful and worthwhile.

There will be peaks and valleys. There will be friends met and friends lost. There will be jobs you love to do and jobs you hate to do. No matter what happens and how you temporarily feel, please never, ever give up on being the amazing bright light that you are. You are lovingly being guided along the way. There is no beginning or end to your JOY. It did not start at your conception; nor will it cease when you leave your physical body. The Journey of You (JOY) is a living, breathing energy that will create a ripple effect within the river of your life.

LETTER TO THE READER

As you read, you will notice periodic references made to a group known as the Mothers Club. The Mothers are women now in spirit who I am able to hear and communicate with psychically. My late mother is one of them. They were my original inspiration for much of the work that I do, as their goal is to help their daughters (and sons) live amazing and fulfilled lives—and that means me and you.

Thank you for choosing to share your JOY with me as you strengthen and grow. Having you read these words now is part of the journey of me, and I will do whatever I can to support you in yours! So with love in your heart, peace in your mind, and joy in your being . . . LET'S IGNITE YOUR JOY!

Deb   xxx

PART I
WHAT'S JOY GOT TO DO WITH IT?

This section is all about getting familiar with what joy truly means to you and why choosing to become familiar with joy has such amazing benefits to all areas of your entire life. Accessing your joy produces a ripple effect that creates positive transformations to the people, experiences, and opportunities that enter your life.

CHAPTER 1
WHY CHOOSE JOY?

"Find a place inside where there's joy, and the joy will burn out the pain."

Joseph Campbell

Why is it so important for us to find our joy? Every human being needs to have the freedom and the privilege to be able to discover her joy so that she may live a life in which she becomes the best version of herself. If you are living the best version of yourself, you are able to give more back to your family, your friends, and your community. You are able to earn an income while doing meaningful work that you love. This concept is the cornerstone to this book. Learning what it is that brings other people joy and assisting them to find ways to get paid for that is something that brings me joy. I believe if everyone chose to live a life that is joyous our world would be a different place.

IGNITE YOUR JOY

Can you imagine how different your life would be if you were living your absolute joy? Can you imagine how differently you might interact with the people at the traffic lights, at the bank, at the local school, in your workplace, and in your family? Then imagine how those people and your family might interact with one another in their workplaces and schools. Wouldn't the world be amazing if they, too, were living a life that was filled with joy? Can you imagine the effect this would have on our world?

I'm passionate about helping people to discover what lights them up and makes their hearts expand, because my version of peace on Earth begins with everyone living her joy at home and in the workplace. That's why I am inviting you to please join me in choosing joy.

As you begin the journey to discover your joy and how you can ignite it, try to remain cool, calm, and collected. Why is this important? So that you do not let your emotions get the better of you. When we are able to stand in an emotional and mental space where our joy is not dependent on external events, we are far more empowered. It helps us to experience life and work in a far more meaningful and joyous way. It allows us to simply be present to life and allow things to unfold miraculously.

Let's say things go your way for a while and you are thrilled, excited, and even ecstatic. Great. Then what happens when the tide turns and things don't

WHY CHOOSE JOY?

go your way? That's when it's important to remain calm. It is also important to be able to gain strength from within, the kind of strength that does not rely on things turning out any specific way. Sometimes things are great and sometimes they are not. Either way, you are the same person inside. With practice, you can find a place where you need not be reliant on anything or anyone for your joy. You will find exercises in this book that will help you practice being comfortable in uncomfortable emotional states as well as more joyful from within rather than from without. There are also exercises that will help you connect to your spiritual self.

It may help you to make a decision to use the external world as a tool for growth. What this means is that within every experience and interaction you have, there is a hidden opportunity. Use it to further your understanding of yourself and the ways in which you interact with the world. Pay close attention to the people and things that "push your buttons," as these are bringing up information from your unconscious that is calling to be recognised, seen, and, if it represents an emotional wound from the past, it may be healed. If you are unable to look at, or process, this information alone, never be afraid to speak to a trusted friend about it. Even better, talk to someone objective such as a mentor, coach, therapist, or alternative healer.

CHAPTER 2
GETTING CLEAR ON WHAT BRINGS YOU JOY

"You were meant to experience a life of joy."

Kay Warren

Getting clear on your destination is the most important step to take in any journey. For if you're unclear as to what you want your life to look like, you'll obviously have no way of knowing how to evaluate if you've created the life you want to live.

Oftentimes we feel that we don't have the right life, so we look for fulfilment outside us. We believe we need new or different—or more—external things to fill our internal gaps. If you ask anyone what it is that she really wants more of in her life, when you drill down far enough into her answers the answer will always be happiness or joy. She may begin by saying she would like to have a bigger house, a yacht, a holiday, or the ability to travel, but when you dig a little deeper by asking, "*Why* the house, yacht, or ability to travel?" the answer generally comes back, "Because I want to *experience* that."

Keep asking, "Why?" and soon you will come to the conclusion that the person believes experiencing the things she's describing will lead her to happiness.

If becoming clear seems like an overwhelming or daunting task right now, let me reassure you that clarity is within your grasp. Inviting more joy into your life is the best way of helping you to discover your true purpose and build a meaningful life and career. It is a way for you to learn more about yourself, the people around you, and your world.

Please trust that your idea of how your life and career should look will become clearer and clearer over time, as you have more experiences to compare against one other. Your idea of what will make you feel joyous may even change as you learn and evolve as a person.

The most important step in this phase of the journey of you is to work out why you do the things you do— to understand why these particular things bring you as much joy as they do, or why you believe and hope they will bring you joy at some point in the future. Interestingly, you don't need to concern yourself yet with how to get anything you envision. It's funny, but if your "why" for doing something is big enough, the "how" usually will take care of itself.

GETTING CLEAR ON WHAT BRINGS YOU JOY

Want a great new job working in the fashion industry? If you're clear about your "why," when the opportunity arises to meet the perfect boss you'll be ready. If you want a promotion at your legal firm, understanding why you want this will help you take the necessary steps to get you this outcome. Let me give you a few examples of someone's big "why" so that you can be very clear on what a "why" is, and does. Examples: A "why" could be:

- To change the way that women are viewed in the workplace (for example, so they may have equal pay as their male colleagues, and will feel safe in balancing their desire for a family with a fulfilling career).

- To set up a charity about which I am deeply passionate.

- To raise awareness about a certain project or issue.

These examples show you that the most motivating "whys" are far bigger than us and our desires and wants. They extend out beyond our families and into our communities, even to the world. Your big "why" can be likened to your legacy (see Chapter 8). What do you want to leave behind when you pass over?

IGNITE YOUR JOY

Is There a Difference Between Joy and Happiness?

Joy and happiness are both emotional states in which a person has feelings of contentment or satisfaction. But these feelings differ based on the reasons causing the feeling and the nature of the feeling. Novelist J.D. Salinger once wrote: "The most singular difference between happiness and joy is that happiness is a solid and joy a liquid."[1] By this, I believe he meant that in the midst of life's ups and downs joy can remain present because it can change shape to adapt to your circumstances.

What to Do When Times Are Tough

Why are you doing what you are doing? Is it because you want to be able to give back? Is it because you want to be able to leave a legacy? Is it simply because you want to experience *this* rather than *that*? If you can become really clear on why you are doing something, this knowledge will enable you to see your way through times that become challenging. Apply the five-step process I will teach you in a few pages. Keep going then, until you feel better.

Winston Churchill once famously said: "If you are going through hell, keep going."[2] Interestingly enough, even though part of you is seeking joy, you may be confronted by other parts of you that are uncomfortable with what you're doing to create joy. At times you may feel extremely unjoyous on the journey of you. If you stay the course during times in which

GETTING CLEAR ON WHAT BRINGS YOU JOY

life seems unjoyous, you'll discover that the joy you experience afterwards is well worth the effort.

The process of gaining clarity about life and career causes many women to feel stress and confusion. After all, if you don't know what you would love to do for a living it can be a major obstacle to doing it.

When we're unclear about what type of work and activities makes us feel valuable, and joyous in our lives, many of us have a tendency to try to please people. We have trouble loving ourselves under these conditions. To get validation from others, as a compensation for lacking our own approval, we can end up putting their expectations of us above expectations that we place on ourselves.

Taking time to identify what you love doing is one of the most important gifts you can offer yourself. For once you're crystal clear on your vision of what brings you joy, you can more easily draw joyful work experiences into your life. Not having clarity is like driving a car wearing a blindfold.

Don't get me wrong, spontaneous living can be care free. And if your career is spontaneously emerging, that is a beautiful thing. But when you keep coming up against the same problems again and again, you know it's time to stop at a gas station and ask for some directions (or at least to turn on your GPS).

IGNITE YOUR JOY

What Does Being Joyful Mean to You?

If you feel stuck in your life and you haven't got the faintest idea of what it is that brings you joy, here is a practical exercise you can do right away to find out. Reflect upon the following four questions and jot down some impressions and insights in a journal for later reference.

- Think back to when you were a child. What did you love to do back then?
- If you could wave a magic wand, what would you have happen in your life?
- If you had all the time and money in the world, how would you spend your days?
- What would you want people to say if they were preparing your eulogy?

The answers to these questions should give you some insight into what it is that you really love to do. Sometimes the answers will be clear and literal, and sometimes they will require more questions in order to make sense of them. For example, if you remember how much you loved dancing as a six-year old girl, but you are currently working as an accountant, does that mean that you should give your four-weeks notice and sign up to join the Australian Ballet? Not necessarily.

What it might mean is that you are missing the

GETTING CLEAR ON WHAT BRINGS YOU JOY

freedom or the feeling that you got from dancing. It may mean that you should sign up for some dance classes so that your inner child can explore those feelings of freedom and joy that she is craving to feel again. Sometimes that is all that is needed to help us recognise what would make us happy today. Sometimes we will need to explore and investigate the world to find that thing we're looking for, and knowing the feeling will guide us.

If you are still stuck and foggy about what you love doing, here are some activities that you can do to help you figure it out.

- **Meditate:** Do this in whatever way you like best. Use a guided meditation app on your phone or touchpad, or just put on some nice music. Or take a class at your local Zen center or yoga studio.

- **Create a vision board:** Cut out images, words, colours, and textures that appeal to you from the pages of magazines. Paste your clippings on a large poster board. Then stop, stand back, and see what "vision" you've created.

- **Invest in sessions with a life coach or therapist:** Get help in brainstorming. Find a professional with whom you can talk out your feelings and ideas, and create strategies.

Clarity makes things flow. Execute the goals you have clarity about, and move on. Create additional

IGNITE YOUR JOY

goals. Execute those. Move on again. Then create more goals. Use this five-step action process to stay on track and keep flowing toward a more joyous life and career.

- **Step 1:** Get clear on your goals.
- **Step 2:** Invent action steps to move toward your goals.
- **Step 3:** Take your action steps.
- **Step 4:** Notice what shows up and how it feels. Are you more or less joyous?
- **Step 5:** Question and analyse your original vision. Is your goal still what you really want? If yes, stick with it. If no, accept that it's no longer what you want and be okay with refining your vision and shifting to a new objective.

The Joy Ride

The journey of you is not a ride for the faint hearted. You may discover moments of sheer, orgasmic bliss and moments of sheer terror on this ride. It has its ups and downs. However, if you are willing to tap into your joy, be prepared for the ride of your life.

Joy is a journey, not a destination. The journey is moving, is flowing, is fluid. No one in the universe can experience your joy. Your joy exists only for you. What brings you joy is yours and yours alone.

GETTING CLEAR ON WHAT BRINGS YOU JOY

Joy is a spiritual experience, an emotional experience, a physical experience, and a mental experience. It is not something given to you by anyone or anything. Finding joy is a discovery process that you enter into when you declare to yourself and the universe that you indeed are ready for your joy. When you do this, magic seems to happen. It is your responsibility to trust your heart and your soul to guide you lovingly to take the journey that you have declared yourself ready for. Making a declaration of this sort may rock the boat, challenge your beliefs, and even bring you to your knees, as it may require you to face your shadow fears. But do not be afraid, for it is in the darker moments that healing occurs, that magic really does happen.

You see, all this time you were perhaps under the impression that joy was something outside of you. Really, it was within you all along. It's through your perception of experiences that you create and experience pleasure or pain.

What if there was no such thing as pleasure or pain; there is no wrong and there is no right. My friend, there just is. There just is!

Your body is your own, your mind is your own, and your heart is your own. Your soul is your own. Your journey to joy, love, connection, ascension, evolution, and knowledge does one thing only: It brings you home.

Welcome home soul, welcome home.

CHAPTER 3

MY JOY STORY
MUM'S THE WORD

"Self-acceptance is nothing more than a shift in consciousness."

Wayne W. Dyer

For as long as I can remember, I felt different because I could sense other people's emotions. One of my earliest memories is of an event that took place at the age of three. It was my first day of preschool. I was holding my mother's hand. Before she even said or did anything, I can recall feeling her anxiety that her baby girl was growing up. I knew she'd have preferred me to continue staying at home. As we approached the door to my new classroom, I looked up and said, "It will be okay, Mummy." She let go of my hand and I walked inside. I knew she was crying in the hallway outside—and why.

That scene has played out a lot in my mind in recent years, especially since my mother's death in

IGNITE YOUR JOY

2008 and the birth of my son five months later, as during this period my intuition and gift for spiritual communication intensified. I used to wonder if it was normal for a girl so young to be as aware of others' feelings as I was. For most of my life, I believed this ability was something every single person shared. I had no idea that it was anything special. As I got older, I alternated between stages of feeling people's emotions intensely and stages of trying to shut them out. I was so sensitive and empathetic that it was often difficult for me to be around people. I got called "overly sensitive," "dramatic," and "weird," so I aimed to block my ability.

I could also feel things around me. In hindsight, I realise that many of the things I sensed were angels, spirit guides, and my ancestors watching over me. Back then, however, sensing them made me freak out. My awakening to my spiritual gifts came at nineteen. I was an undergraduate psychology student back then, working at a hotel bar for pocket money. It was 2 A.M., cold and rainy, and I'd just come home from a shift at the bar. Exhausted and smelling like coffee, smoke, and alcohol, I was unable to relax, let alone sleep. Two weeks earlier I'd broken up with the boy who was my first love. My life felt shattered. I felt like I'd never smile again . . . like the sun would never shine again. I didn't know what to do with myself and my black mood.

Then I had a sudden urge to write. Not knowing

what else to do at that hour, I grabbed a pen and notebook and began:

Dear Diary,

I hate myself. I hate life. Everything sucks. I feel like the sun will never shine again. I hate love. I don't want to feel this way. I'd rather feel numb than feel anything at all.

After a rather rambling pity party, I then asked a question that was to open up Pandora's Box for me. It was neither self-aware nor enlightened. It even had the "F" word thrown in. The beautiful thing about my question was that it set me on a journey back to myself that has continued since that cold and rainy night. I simply asked:

How the f--- did I get here?"

This question elicited a response for which I was unprepared—at least on a conscious level. The answer was:

You are exactly where you are supposed to be, my angel. Everything is working out just perfectly.

As my hand began to write this remark down on paper, I didn't give myself a moment to think. I just let what was happening happen. I let go. I continued writing. As I did, I knew I was writing, but it was unconscious. It felt like I wasn't doing the writing, but that something or someone else was using my body to express itself. My hand was simply holding the pen.

Although I really had no idea what the message coming through was, I sensed it was amazing. After what felt like hours and seconds both, my hand stopped, put down the pen it was holding, and closed the notebook. I was utterly gobsmacked. Speechless. (If you knew me you'd understand how amazing this speechlessness was in and of itself.)

After a minute or two, I reopened the notebook. Feeling curious and a little frightened, I read:

> *We are your guides, Debbie. It is so lovely of you to make contact with us in this lifetime. We're so happy to connect with you again. We've worked with you over thousands of years and many lifetimes. We have always been here and will always be here. We love you unconditionally and we're here to support and guide you through your journey.*

Okaaaay, I thought, *I've gone insane!* I shut the book again quickly and threw it on the floor as if it was a pair of someone else's dirty socks. Then, trembling and weak at the knees, I ran and woke up my mother. By this time it was somewhere between four and five in the morning, so I wasn't thinking straight. "Mum,

MY JOY STORY MUM'S THE WORD

Mum, wake up!" I said. "Something is really badly wrong with me!"

My dear mother was always like a mama lioness watching her cubs. Even though I was nineteen by then and my brother was twenty-three, married, and living out of the family home, Mum was still our lioness. When she heard my voice, she jumped out of bed and looked me up and down. "Where? Why? How? What happened?"

Realising I'd given her a fright and was being incredibly selfish, I apologised and explained what had happened. Keep in mind that I was studying psychology at university, so I was quick to "diagnose" myself. The week prior we'd learned about a number of mental illnesses in class. I was upset because I thought the notebook proved I was becoming schizophrenic.

Mum accompanied me back to my room where I pointed at the notebook like it had evil powers. With her encouragement, I slowly picked it up and reluctantly began to read the words I'd written just a few minutes earlier.

Reading the words the second time around, I relaxed. I felt easier and lighter with each breath I took and every word I read. I continued until I'd read forty handwritten pages aloud while Mum sat on my bed, listening intently. When I finished, we looked at each other and smiled. "Maybe I'm not crazy," I said to Mum.

"Oh, Deb. Where did I get you from, ladybug?" she answered with a grin on her tired face.

We decided after a short discussion that I probably wasn't "crazy," but that I was either A) very imaginative, or B) a spiritual teacher.

The second possibility seemed unlikely to either of us at that time.

I felt reassured because my mother was confident that I wasn't "being controlled" or "harming myself or others," which are two of the symptoms that psychologists use to diagnose schizophrenia.

During her life, Mum was my number one supporter. She didn't understand most of the things I did, like obsessing about my boyfriends and my habit of analysing every word said to me. While alive, she didn't understand my connection to the guides that were working with me (and have been "over thousands of years and many lifetimes"). She nevertheless believed me when I told her that the unconscious writing I did in my notebook came from them, not me. She knew I wasn't someone to lie, fib, or make things up.

Mum always used to say, "I don't understand it, Deb, but I believe you."

After my awakening that night in 1999, a full-blown spiritual quest began in my life. It upstaged many of my other activities and involved buying and reading any and every book I could find that was mystical and esoteric. I read about channelling, energy fields, angels, fairies, and past lives. My bedroom walls were covered in affirmations. I did angel card readings for myself and my family and friends. I immersed myself in a world that was far more interesting and reliable than the physical world seemed to be, and my spirit guides and the angels (and occasionally the spirits of dead people) were always hanging around ready either to entertain or to support me.

Quite frankly, it was a miracle I earned two university degrees. But I did.

After school, I held different jobs. For a while I was a social worker. Then I entered the fashion world. My intuition always played a big role in how I operated, but being a spiritual teacher wasn't my career . . . yet.

Defending Your Life

Mum lost her father, my grandfather, back in 1962 when she was just fifteen and her little sister was only six. She held so much anger at her "daddy leaving" that she couldn't make sense of a lot of her life. Sadly, my beautiful mother therefore carried a broken heart to her deathbed. I never understood how badly she must have felt until she died and my own heart broke. I took a vow the day Mum died that I'd do my absolute best not to carry the pain that the grief had injected my heart with. I didn't want my unborn son (who was only a tiny foetus in my tummy at the time) to feel the sadness I felt.

Once Mum was gone, I was not only grieving for the death of my mother, but for her grief at losing the grandfather I had never known and other emotional wounds that Mum was unable to heal during her life.

Despite Mum's lack of belief, we had often discussed the afterlife. Sometimes we'd stay up past midnight and chat about it. I'd tell her about my communication with people who had crossed over. They often showed me modes of transportation, like buses and trains, to explain what transitioning between life and death was like. One night the movie *Defending Your Life* came on TV and it was incredibly affirming. To this day this is one of my favourite movies. It stars Meryl Streep and Albert Brooks as two people who fall in love after meeting in a transit dimension.

Mum and I nearly fell off the couch in a scene where the main character arrives at a place called Judgment City. Bus/train vehicles are everywhere and all newly arrived "passengers" are being sorted into the appropriate car for their level of soul development. Neither of us had expected to watch this flick, and it couldn't have been timed more perfectly if we'd tried.

Mum loved movies. In particular, really old movies. Thus, I grew up watching Lucille Ball, Jerry Lewis, and Dean Martin. I suffered through the golden oldie tunes Mum had on in the car. My brother and I would tease her for singing hilarious old songs like "Tie a Yellow Ribbon 'Round the Old Oak Tree" by Tony Orlando and Dawn and the even older "I've Got a Lovely Bunch of Coconuts" sung by the talk show host Merv Griffin of all people! What made these songs seem so hysterical to us were not just the terrible lyrics, but the fact that Mum (and I love you, Mum) had the absolute worst voice I've ever heard.

The reason for the back story here is that Mum would always sing or hum the same song when she saw a train in a movie. This song was "Chattanooga Choo Choo." As we watched *Defending Your Life* that night, that's what she was humming. I turned to her and joked, "Hey, that song should be our sign for when you're gone so that I know you're okay 'up there.'"

My Mother Crosses Over

At 6:37 P.M. on Tuesday, April 15, 2008, I got a call from my brother, who said, "Mum had a stroke. She's okay, but she's in hospital." My husband, Ben, and I hopped into the car. As we drove to see Mum, I was scared, though not shocked that she was ill. I figured that all the stress she'd put herself under for years from lack of self-care had led her body to fight back. Mum's body was screaming at her, pleading with her, "Love me! Help me!"

IGNITE YOUR JOY

I grew up in a close-knit Jewish family in Melbourne, Australia. Mum was my best friend. I loved and admired her, but she also had a way of pushing my buttons. You see, her life consisted of taking care of me and my brother, my dad, her younger sister, and my gorgeous grandmother, Nanna. That was it. We were her reason for being. We were her life. If we were okay, then she was okay.

Mum was warm and nurturing. If you were lucky enough to be in, or connected to, our family, you received all of her incredible love and generosity, and felt truly mothered. She was our rock, our anchor, and the glue that stuck everything together. She was the one you rang when things went pear shaped, or brilliantly. She was everything to us. But she didn't take care of herself.

Recent months were traumatic for Mum. Nanna developed vascular dementia and was slowly becoming someone else. Mum and her sister were caring for her 24/7, but Nanna really needed more than their attention. She needed professional care. That was stressful. Mum also had diabetes, although she'd kept this a secret from the family for five years. Also, a few months earlier she'd fallen down a flight of stairs and broken an ankle. It had to be put into a cast, making Mum wheelchair-bound. It was only a week before the stroke that Mum could walk again.

I wish the story ended there. I wish I could tell you that Mum went on to rehab and ended up changing her life, living happier and healthier. I wished. I prayed. Surely God wouldn't take away a mother when her daughter was four months pregnant with her first child? Surely that wouldn't be fair? But God took her. Mum died and left our family behind. My son was a grandchild she was never to meet—at least not on Earth. Like a bus leaving just as you're running to catch it, he was coming in as she was going out.

It turned out that Mum's stroke was triggered by advanced liver cancer. She lived another eighteen days in the hospital. For those eighteen days, the family loved her, fed her, talked to her, hugged her, and kissed her. We said our goodbyes. Then she left the world peacefully.

A Message from My Mother

I realise that as a spiritual teacher I am blessed to connect with spirits on the other side, both for myself and for other people. On May 20, approximately ten minutes after her passing, I got my first message of this sort from my mother. She said, "Deb, it's all right. It will be okay. You will be all right. I promise!"

It was very moving and I was crying. I could feel Mum moving away from me and saw a visual of her looking out toward a train station with a lot of action on the platform. Then, Mum cursed. She said, "Bugger it!" Apparently she'd taken a wrong turn and didn't know where to go.

I could also sense her surprise that some of us in the family had been right: There actually is an afterlife. She was also surprised that we were right that if you don't take care of yourself your body dies. Mum was in shock that she was dead!

At 4:24 A.M., Mum woke me up from my sleep, asking, "Am I really dead, Deb?"

"Yes," I said.

"I'm okay. I just can't really believe it. I'm glad you can hear me. No one else can. I tried to speak to everyone." She continued, "I'm here with the family," and went on to list some of our ancestors who were there with her. It was lovely for me because, as she said their names, I saw them, too. "I wish we could all be together, Deb, but I know we can't right now."

Mum showed me an image in my mind's eye of herself embracing her father. She looked pretty and young with dark hair and a slim physique. To me she looked how she did when my brother and I were younger, as she did in her mid thirties. Her father also looked very young; he seemed to be around the same age.

Mum then showed me an image of her sitting at a desk with a counsellor or administrator of some kind. He was showing her a form that described her life. It had details on it, including a line that read: "Upper Age Limit 68." Mum explained to me that everyone has an "end date," like the expiration date on a carton of milk. This is the maximum age that they could live to in their current lifetime. Mum's was sixty-eight, but she had died at sixty-one because she didn't take care of herself. She was never meant to live past that date. No matter how well she'd treated her body, she'd never have become a great-grandmother with grey hair living in a nursing home.

My mother had come to Earth to raise a family and teach us how to love—and she did. On a soul level, Mum was content knowing her children were with loving partners and happy in their lives. She left knowing she was a grandmother. Although she would have liked to meet the baby on Earth, she couldn't hold on that long.

She told me, "Really I never would have wanted to be an old, old lady anyway. I hated growing old." She also explained she had chosen her death and its timing before she was born. She had wanted her death to be as quick and pain free as possible, but also long enough that she and her family could say a proper goodbye.

Mum gave me messages she wanted passed on to the rest of the family. She started with my brother. "Please tell him, 'I'm so proud of you, my big boy. You did such a good job. You are so strong and you did everything and so much more than a son should do. I love you so much.'" Mum was referring to the amazing job my brother and his wife had done in caring for her during her final days. As Mum told me this, I could feel her putting both hands on my brother's face. The image she showed me was of her hugging him and kissing his cheeks.

In the morning, at the funeral, I would do exactly this to my brother's face as I gave him the message. I believed Mum wanted him to feel her through me.

Mum then explained to me that every night before my brother and I fell asleep from then on she would come and kiss us goodnight. She emphasized the words *Every. Single. Night.* I felt Mum kiss me as she said this. I felt a kiss on my cheek and then a kiss on my neck that tickled me. Mum always used to do that and it annoyed me. Again, in a cheeky way, she said, "Every night and whenever I want to . . . and you can't stop me."

Mum then had a message for my dad. "Debbie, please tell your father that I am healed. Please tell him that I am sorry. I know how much and how hard he tried to get me to be healed. I know all about his meditations and prayers, and the times he pleaded with God, and with me, to be okay. Tell him I am. I am only sorry that I couldn't be healed in the way that he meant for me to be. But I am healed! And I love him very, very much . . . and always will.

"Please tell him that I want him to be happy. I want

him to move on. I do not want him to hang on to things like I did. If he wants to throw something out or do whatever he wants to do, then I want him to. I won't be mad with him. I don't care anymore. I realise it was all rubbish.

"Tell him that he's going to meet someone. I will make sure of that. I don't want him to be alone for too long, so I am going to make sure that he isn't. We are up here conspiring as to how, when, and who. Tell him I know that although I didn't really believe in this 'mumbo-jumbo,' now that I'm here I know that it's real. Therefore I can guide and help him every step of the way in his life from now on . . . and I'm going to. Tell him that I'll be his little angel, watching over him sitting on his right shoulder whenever he needs me."

I got an image of Dad at a class or a support group meeting and had the impression from Mum that it was important for Dad to follow his intuition, because that was going to be how he started a new life for himself romantically and professionally. Not that he would literally meet someone at a class necessarily, but that if he got out there and did things it would lead to meeting new people and having new experiences. These would ultimately lead him to have a new life.

The message for my aunty was: "My little one, I'm sorry. I know how hard it is for you that I'm gone and I'm so sorry. Please know that you are going to get through this . . . just like we did everything else. You have to know that you're stronger than you realise. Think about everything you've been through and let it make you stronger."

Mum then went on to talk to her sister about moving my grandmother into an aged care facility. She said things she never would have said when she was alive, like: "It's okay for her to be in a home. I see things differently from up here." She also passed on a greeting from her father, "Daddy says hi. He is so proud of us. He was with us the whole time!"

Mum grew adamant. "Now listen, Mum [meaning, Nanna] is going to be okay and you are going to be okay. I don't want you doing what I did. You are supposed to be there longer to watch your kids grow up and meet your grandchildren. Please don't do what I did. I was stupid to neglect my health. Don't copy 'stupid.' Learn from my mistakes. If you can't do it for yourself, then please do it for me. Don't drive yourself into the ground trying to take care of Mum. You won't be able to; she's only going to get worse."

She continued, "I've had a look at some pamphlets the kids got hold of about homes for her. One is very nice. It's elegant and Mum will like it. It's fine if you need to do your research to find the best one, but it's going to end up being this one. By the way, her illness is a blessing in disguise. She's had enough crap in her lifetime and she doesn't need to know I am dead."

MY JOY STORY MUM'S THE WORD

Everything Mum said about my grandmother would come true.

Toward the end of our conversation, I told Mum that we all wanted to know where she'd stashed her jewellery. Mum's jewellery was very special, as my grandfather had been a jeweller. A lot of her pieces were his designs. Mum said, "I don't know if I can even remember. Oh no, wait. It's in the bedroom in the antique cupboard in some boxes. Don't let your father throw any of that stuff out . . . and get your brother to look through it! He's more careful than you are."

Me and my brother would look for the jewellery a few days later and it was exactly where she'd said it would be. My brother, being careful, unwrapped something hidden inside a tissue in a medicine jar inside the boxes that I was about to throw out. Thank goodness we'd listened to Mum. Inside was a diamond engagement ring that she'd saved.

Before her funeral, I passed along the messages Mum had given me to deliver. As sad as I was that I wouldn't be able to touch her and be with her in person from then on, it gave me great comfort that I could feel her presence with me and that we could communicate so clearly. What a blessing!

My Angel Mother

During the year following her death, my mother regularly connected with me. It didn't ease my loss entirely; however I was grateful to sense her presence with me when I was giving birth to my son and after. My labour was long and difficult, yet I felt protected spiritually by Mum. My husband, Ben, was by my side supporting me in the delivery room, and together we became such proud parents. That was a very joyful day for us, with Mum cheering me on from the other side. I had already decided to stop working in order to stay home with the baby.

The first hint I had that my mother had a special purpose, one I could play a role in, came when I took a trip to Sydney to visit a friend of mine. I took my son and we went to stay as houseguests with her and her three kids for several days. One night, after the kids were asleep, we sat down for a conversation. As I spoke with my friend, in my mind's eye I saw my mother and my girlfriend's mother (also deceased) having coffee together at a round table. Sunlight was streaming through a window behind them. It just looked like living women catching up with one another, having a chat about their husbands and kids. There were three or four other empty chairs at the table.

The next day, I had an urge to go and visit the house my friend grew up in. It wasn't far away, so we hopped in the car and went over the next morning. Let me tell you, I almost fell over when we got to the house.

MY JOY STORY MUM'S THE WORD

As we walked into the kitchen, right before my eyes I saw the same round table with the sun streaming through the window behind it that I'd seen in my vision the night before.

You might not expect someone like me to judge her own abilities as a spiritual teacher or channel, but I did and sometimes still do. That was a huge sign that made me realise something was going on that my mother wanted to bring to my attention. As several weeks went by, she kept showing me a similar image of the table, but the room kept getting bigger, the table kept getting bigger, and there were more chairs around the table—and the scene expanded until there were hundreds or even thousands of previously empty chairs beginning to be filled. That's what I was seeing and I knew there was a reason for it.

There was a particular day that made me realise I was connected to something profound. I'd dropped my son off at the day care center and I decided to have a day off for myself, though I didn't have a plan. *Where shall I go?* I thought and ended up going into a shop that sold lighting. I walked in and found that it was not my style, but older, more antique stuff. As I was turning around to leave I felt the presence of my mother holding me back. *Okay, I'll stay,* I thought and began chatting with the shop assistant. Right away I felt the presence of her mother around her, too. I'd never done a reading for a stranger before, but since I was feeling this presence so strongly I decided to ask her if her mum had passed away. She had.

IGNITE YOUR JOY

I told the shopkeeper that I saw her mum sitting at the table with my mum and my friend's mum. The woman was sipping a cup of tea. The shop assistant said, "Oh, she loved her cuppa!" We talked for a while and cried together. Even though it was a lovely experience, by the time I walked out of the store I was overwhelmed. It was new for me to connect so strongly with a departed loved one and have the information confirmed by a complete stranger.

I knew I needed to do something to relax before picking up my son. As I was driving along I noticed I was passing a swanky day spa that I'd been to before. A parking spot was open right outside the front door. I grabbed it. "I haven't got a booking," I said to the lady at the front desk, "but I really need a massage. Do you have anyone available for a quick twenty minutes?" It was a peak time and they were booked up, with the exception of a therapist named Stacy (not her real name) who just happened to have a half hour open. "I'll put you with her," the receptionist said.

As I sat down to wait for Stacy, again I felt the energy of a deceased woman around me. I got up and went back to the desk and said, "This question is going to sound bizarre, but has anyone here recently lost her mother?" Then I explained that I was a medium. With tears in her eyes the woman said, "Yes, Stacy, the one I booked you with. She lost her mum six months ago."
I didn't end up having the massage. Instead I connected to Stacy's mum for thirty minutes and did

a reading for Stacy. It was profound—probably the most profound reading I've ever given, in fact—even though it was only the second reading I ever gave. I did my first and second readings for strangers on the same day—that day! My mother and the mothers of my girlfriend, the shop assistant, and the massage therapist had connected me to Stacy for a professional reason as well as a personal reason for me and for them. Being able to connect is a beautiful blessing, as it allows us to know that our loved ones really are okay and still watching over us.

My mother gave me a sign that I should become a professional medium in November 2009. I was in the spare room in our house where Ben and I store miscellaneous belongings. I remember looking for an item of clothing for my son, who was one at the time. As I walked past a book shelf, a book literally dropped on my foot. I hadn't even touched the shelf, so already I knew this was an important book that I was meant to read. I looked down and saw that it was *Crossing Over* by the famous medium John Edward, who used to host a show on TV by that name.

My first thought was, *Do I own this book?* I knew my husband didn't because his book collection consists of books on law, history, and military campaigns, and comic books. Though I knew it had to be mine, I had no idea of when or where I bought it.

After I picked the book off my right foot I turned to the page it was opened to: "Chapter 2: My Three

Signs." At that stage I wasn't particularly impressed. Let me tell you, I come from a background in psychology and a family composed of extremely intelligent, left-brained individuals. It takes something big for me to believe an event is not a coincidence. I figured that John Edward, who is a world-class medium, was going to discuss a client of his who got signs from a loved one. But I turned the page and skimmed the chapter until I came to a passage that read: "It was the experience surrounding my mother's passing . . ."

"Okay," I said to my spirit guides and Mum, "you've got my full attention."

I liked John Edward and had watched his show, *Crossing Over*, several times. He was a gifted, genuine psychic-medium. But I had never known that his mother had passed away. After reading that line, I made myself a cup of tea, checked that the boys (my son and my hubby) were okay, and then I began to read the book in earnest from the beginning.

Back at "Chapter 2: My Three Signs" I began to feel sad as I read about John missing his mother. It reminded me of how sad I'd felt at my own mum's funeral. I continued reading, feeling awful, and regretting Mum's absence, when, all of a sudden, a piece of paper fell out of the book. It was folded four times over and flattened, and it looked like it had been nestled in that book for a long while.

MY JOY STORY MUM'S THE WORD

To be honest, the fact that the paper fell out was as odd as the book falling on my foot. I hadn't even turned a page when it dropped into my lap. I was too deep in thought. I unfolded the paper and opened it to find a note written in my own messy handwriting. I turned icy cold and was flooded by emotions at the sight of it. Tears began to stream down my face. The note read: "Pardon me boys, is that the Chattanooga Choo Choo?"

After that day, I decided to test the waters as a medium and to do my best to help other people who had lost their loved ones find peace, just as John Edward does. Mum helped me get started and so did the other mothers she was hanging around with. In 2011, I set up a business called Unlock Your Best Life with which I was blessed enough to do angel card readings, medium connections, and life purpose readings. I thought that I was on my journey of joy and that this was my life's work. However, as I learned . . . life is always a "to be continued" adventure.

I ended up setting up another business in 2013, a partnership that lasted only six months. Amazing lessons and connections were made (both in the earthly realm and the spiritual realm) during that short period in my professional career.

In 2014, I decided it was time to just be Debbie. I launched DebbieZita.com, a website announcing my work as a spiritual teacher and business coach. What the future holds, well, we will have to wait and see. And in case you're wondering, ". . . But I thought you were psychic and therefore know your future?" Let me tell you, it doesn't work that way. Even spiritual teachers and psychics don't know our future.

I personally don't believe in reading fortunes. I believe in helping people create them.

PART II
LOVE, LOSS, AND THE CYCLE OF LIFE

In order to be able to make sense of our own JOY, it helps to know that even the toughest times in life are part of the evolutionary process. I know this all too well after losing Mum. It takes time and a willingness to learn, grow, and let go.

Fortunately, you can move on from painful times and allow them to propel you even more rapidly forward along your journey toward having the life and career of your dreams.

CHAPTER 4
CHOOSE LOVE OVER FEAR

"When we are afraid, we pull back from life. When we are in love, we open to all that life has to offer with passion, excitement, and acceptance."

John Lennon

In order for a person to really comprehend something, she must also comprehend its opposite. In order to experience warmth, she must experience cold. To experience the light, she needs to experience the darkness. The same goes for pain and pleasure, connectedness and disconnectedness, and so on.

You get the picture.

What about love?

What emotion is the opposite of love?

IGNITE YOUR JOY

Many people assume the opposite of love is hate, when in fact, it is fear.

If you've been walking a spiritual path for a while, this idea that love and fear go hand in hand is probably not new to you. In my experience, love and fear are also related to the soul and the ego. The ego fears, whereas the soul loves.

Experiencing the polarity of fear/ego is an important part of the human journey. Although fearful and ego-driven experiences are often given a bad rap, they are crucial to us—not only because they teach us to recognise and appreciate love, but also because they are a means of keeping us safe and protected. Think about how much you appreciate a warm woolly jumper in the middle of winter or an ice-cold glass of water in the middle of summer. Going through (or as I like to say *growing through*) fear gives you a newfound respect and appreciation for the love that is about to enter your life and be found in your heart.

Fear plays a part in keeping us alive. It helps to protect us from predators. The psychological reflex we have when facing danger is known as the fight-or-flight response. Just as a hyena would go on high alert when facing a lion, so too, do we, if we are approached by a mugger in a dark alley. The body releases high levels of cortisol and adrenaline in order to prepare for what it needs to do when threatened. This is crucial in stressful situations, but dangerous if we stay in a state of hyper alertness for too long. It's

CHOOSE LOVE OVER FEAR

also not usually necessary in business meetings or social settings; nonetheless, we often drop into the fight-or-flight mode at such times.

The modern world seems to be in a perpetual state of tension and fear, as the body never gets a sufficient opportunity to recover between bouts of stress. This begs the question: How do we begin to overcome this? We first need to recognise that although this mode is normal—in that it is commonplace—this mode is detrimental to our minds, bodies, and spirits. Also, it's detrimental to our careers. For example, if we have been invited to make a professional presentation, being afraid can hold us back and prevent us from impressing or influencing our listeners in the way this opportunity otherwise might allow us. Fear can hold us back from trying new things or entering unfamiliar settings that would teach us more about what we love to do and the path our soul is destined to take.

One of the most beautiful things you can do for your mind, body, and soul is to recognise when you are stressed and find ways to reduce that stress.

You may have already noticed that stress creates more stress. Similarly, love creates more love. So, whenever possible, replace a thought that makes you feel stressed with a thought that makes you feel loving. A great example of this might be walking into a store where you are greeted by a salesperson with a smile versus a sales person who is oblivious to your existence. In this case, the joyful greeting might inspire you to spend time and money in that store as opposed to walking out immediately. The experience created here might be a great day in sales for the salesperson versus a quiet day.

Another great example (which was actually experienced by one of my coaching clients) was taking the owner of a legal firm for coffee to discuss the possibility of rebranding the firm. The result was the lawyer signing up for my client's most valuable branding package. My client had already had a meeting with the owner's marketing director and been told, "I think your service is too pricey." After that exchange occurred, I encouraged him to play a love game. I asked him, "Ideally, what would you love to see happen in this situation? What would you *love* to do for this law firm?" He said he would love to rebrand the company. Hearing this I made the suggestion of taking the owner of the business for coffee so the owner could explain to my client what he really needed and wanted to get out of the rebranding experience.

The most important thing was my last bit of advice: I said, "If you feel that you can really help him and his legal firm, then please let him know that. After you do, be okay with whatever choice the lawyer makes." The rest, as they say, is history.

Choose to love!

CHOOSE LOVE OVER FEAR

De-stress, de-clutter, "de-fear" your life. Do your best to live in peaceful child-like wonder. Find ways to bring more harmony, balance, and integration into your life and the world around you, and ways to bring them into your being, expressing them inwardly. How does fear show up for you? Know your emotional and physical responses and design a plan that is your personal equivalent of the sign: "In case of emergency, break glass." Stress symptoms are different for everyone.

Here are two practical ways you can turn fear into love and stress into peace.

1. Be absolutely certain of how your body demonstrates stress. Does your heart beat faster? Do you perspire? Does your mind go blank? Get to know in great detail what your specific body does, so that you can recognise the state of stress. Stress symptoms are different for everyone.

2. Make a Stress Prevention Plan, a list of all the things that make you feel better almost instantly. This is something that I was taught when I was in hospital suffering from post-natal depression (PND) and severe anxiety. This list can be an invaluable tool, as your brain literally shuts off its thinking processes when it is feeling stressed, so that the memory is affected.

IGNITE YOUR JOY

Creating Your Stress Prevention Plan

Here's how to create a customised Stress Prevention Plan.

1. In a calm and relaxed state, get out a notebook or a piece of paper and pen, or open a new file on your computer.

2. Name your document My Stress Prevention Plan.

3. Write a list of at least ten things that bring you an almost instant sense of peace. The simpler the instructions, the better.

4. Keep this list somewhere that you can easily access it. We tend to forget the list even exists unless we are feeling stressed.

5. When you are feeling anxious or stressed, pull out the document and pick one thing to do from the list. You may not feel like doing any of them, but do something anyway. Pick the most appealing idea (or if you are feeling really shitty, pick the least irritating one).

6. If you are still feeling a bit off, keep doing things from the list until you feel better. You may not end up feeling quite 100 percent of your usual self, but that is okay. You will feel better than you did. Stress prevention is not a magic pill (I do not know of one). But this exercise should

CHOOSE LOVE OVER FEAR

bring you to a place where you are feeling better and able to sit with your feelings and or get on with the jobs that might be required to keep your life going.

Tip 1: Place a note or a reminder somewhere that says, "In case of emergency, read My Stress Prevention Plan. This is a play on the classic phrase: "In case of emergency break glass." Put this note somewhere that you are likely to look when you are stressed, such as on top of your wine rack. You might put a duplicate note in the freezer next to the chocolate ice cream. Eventually you won't need a reminder at all. You'll know exactly what to do to feel better.

Tip 2: While you are in a calm state it is a great idea to ask yourself the following questions:

- What does stress feel like in my body? For example, heart beating faster than normal, dizziness, and so on.

- What thoughts do I often think when I am stressed? For example, "This is hopeless," "I suck," "I am worthless."

- What do I tend to do while I am stressed? For example, I eat more, I eat less, I ring a friend to talk, or I masturbate (although this may seem strange, it is common, as it is a way to relieve pent-up energy).

IGNITE YOUR JOY

Use these questions to start becoming more aware of yourself. Then, when stress does visit, you are super clear that it is present.

Here is my own Stress Prevention Plan. Feel free to adopt it or use it as a guide however you like as you design your own customised plan. Some of these things are appropriate to do at work while others you can only do in the privacy of your own home.

When I am stressed, I will:

- Drink a cup of peppermint tea.
- Breathe: Inhale for five counts, hold for five counts, then exhale for five counts. Repeat the sequence at least five times.
- Go for a walk.
- Listen to uplifting music (for me its Beyoncé and Ani Difranco).
- Go outside and walk barefoot on the grass.
- Take a shower or a bath with relaxing oils or gels.
- Use sprays or oils that smell yummy to me. (I use aura soma quintessence and energy clearing spray by Infinite U.)
- Play with angel cards (or any oracle deck or book with pretty words and images).

CHOOSE LOVE OVER FEAR

- Paint. (Although I am far from talented, I love looking at the colours and focusing on putting my emotions on paper.)

- Write.

- Watch inspiring videos such as videos by Marianne Williamson and Abraham-Hicks.

- Watch a comedy show.

- Chat with a trusted, non-biased friend or therapist. Another great resource, if you are in Australia, is LifeLine. They are a high-quality, twenty-four-hour counselling service for anyone in a crisis; just dial 131114. In the United States and the United Kingdom, a similar organisation is the Samaritans.

- Meditation: I like to use the following guided audios:

    > *Open Heart Meditation* by Irmansyah Effendi,
    > *Chakra Rebalancing* by Doreen Virtue,
    > Anything by Louise Hay,
    > Anything by Glenn Harold.

- Get a massage or pedicure/manicure.

- Reorganise a room or a cupboard, if you feel good doing so.

- Read something light and funny.

- Go shopping, while being careful to limit the amount you spend. (This advice is twofold:

IGNITE YOUR JOY

First, you are vulnerable, so you could spend a lot quite easily; second, you probably will not like what you buy as it will contain the energy of the stress period. Best to save the big shop for another time.)

"Imagine that your soul is made up of ten parts. One-tenth of it is your human spirit. Nine-tenths is your spirit's spirit. We want you to know that even though the larger part of our souls goes on to evolve, there is always one-tenth that will forever remain your mother. Although the soul is not attached to the physical anymore, we still love and care for our families on Earth.

"Before you came to Earth, you met with your guides and the spirits of your parents-to-be. At this meeting, you discussed the lessons your soul wished to learn. In order for you to learn, you appointed characters in your life. Both you and your various characters made a contract that binds your souls together. Once a lesson has been dealt, you as a human/spirit have a choice. Free will is the reason. You may either choose to respond with love or fear. If you are able to respond with love you are acting from your soul. If you choose to act out of fear, you

are acting from your ego, your human self. We say this without judgment. Every soul and person can always choose again. Let us remind you that, as your mothers, we love you no matter what choices you make."

The Mothers' Club

From the work I have done with the Mothers' Club, I have learned that our deceased loved ones still love and care for their families on Earth. They especially care for the well-being of their children. The mother-child bond is the strongest of any. A mother's love for her child really could move mountains and so is everlasting. No amount of time and space can ever change the love a mother has for her child.

The language of love is recognisable in every part of the world and in the animal kingdom. Imagine if we could spend our time living in that beautiful energy we call love. Given the state of the world we live in, it does not seem to be the case. It seems we spend a majority of our time living in fear rather than in a state of love. Love and fear are the only two emotions that exist. Every other emotion stems from one of these. This is quite a simple notion to comprehend on an intellectual level. It is another thing to be able to choose love over fear in an emotional or spiritual sense.

IGNITE YOUR JOY

The concept of love versus fear can also be understood as the soul versus the ego. The ego fears, whereas the soul loves. It is important to remember that the soul is a part of the Divine and all things divine are made up of 100 percent pure love. Therefore love is an energetic aspect of us that we should try to draw upon during times of immense stress, adversity, and trauma. Often referred to as the "strength of the human spirit," the soul exists inside each and every one of us.

The soul is physically located within every cell in our bodies, and energetically radiates to every part of our auric field. Recognised as a state of peace, calm, and absolute knowing, it can be accessed during deep meditation or dreaming, and through physical activities such as lovemaking and childbirth. When we're operating from our souls, it feels like everything is moving in sync and makes sense. There is a feeling of ease and peace, as well as absolute trust.

The following exercise can give you an experience of soulful love.

The Love Exercise

A way to access the soul/love part of yourself is to close your eyes and take three deep breaths in through your nose and out through your mouth. On every in-breath, imagine calm and peace entering your being. On every out-breath feel the stress that has built up being released.

After taking three breaths in and out, feel the love that you hold in your heart for your family. This works really well if you can imagine your children, even your unborn children or a pet (remember, the love is not coming from them, but from the Divine). As you breathe in love for whomever you are imagining in your mind, notice how and what you are feeling, and where sensations are occurring in your body. You may begin to notice that your heart rate has slowed down. You may be overcome with emotions of love and joy. You may feel like your heart has opened up and expanded, and that you are easily giving and receiving divine love with this person. A feeling of completeness or peace may wash over you.

All these feelings are feelings of love. This is the divine feeling of your soul or true essence—or that which you call by any other name you like. (A rose by any other name would still smell as sweet.)

Now that we have discussed, and even embodied, love, it is important to do the same for fear.

The Fear Exercise

We can only know the light by also experiencing the darkness. Therefore, I will walk you through an exercise to embody your fears. Again, as we did in

IGNITE YOUR JOY

the Love Exercise, close your eyes and take three deep breaths in and out. This time, however, instead of imagining your loved ones, I want you to imagine a stressful or tense situation. I ask you to imagine a situation as opposed to an actual person, as this exercise is not about judging anyone or anything.

In your mind's eye, focus on the stressful situation you've chosen. It may be a relationship breakup, career confusion, or something that makes you feel powerless, like a power outage or traffic. Really allow yourself to believe it is happening to you in the present moment. Notice what, where, and how you are feeling stress. Has your heart rate increased? Does it feel like your heart has closed? Maybe you feel like you have tension in your head, back, or stomach? I personally feel stress in my solar plexus. You could feel as if you have an energetic wall around you (like you need protection). Of course, you may feel none or a combination of these things. None is a right or wrong way to feel. Everything just is as it is.

Now, let's bring you back to a place of love. Let's take you out of the fearful or tense situation you have visited. Imagine yourself watching that tense situation as a movie. Remove any emotion by watching the scene in your mind's eye as a spectator and not as a participant.

After you have studied the scene, see yourself floating above the scene and move yourself to another place, one that brings you peace. It can help to imagine yourself in a picturesque setting like a park or on the shore of an ocean.

You can also do the Love Exercise again to bring yourself back to a place of calm.

The Difference Between Fear and Healthy Discomfort

These two very simple exercises of identifying love and fear are a brilliant way for you to measure how you are feeling about a person or a situation—even one that's only prospective and in the future, such as a job interview or a date with someone new. Of course, many times anticipation of something unknown can make us anxious in a way that would stop us from growing appropriately. So how we can tell the difference between real fear that can protect us from real danger and the kind of fear that is not useful (False Evidence Appearing Real)?

Is fear ever useful other than when we're facing life-threatening danger?

I know, for myself, that I am feeling love any time I meet someone or enter a new situation in which my heart feels open, receptive, and calm. If, on the other hand, my heart feels constricted and closed, then that is a sign of fear. Here is where it can get confusing. I often hear people say: "I'm not sure if I'm

IGNITE YOUR JOY

feeling fearful or just uncomfortable."

How can you feel the difference between being fearful and just being out of your comfort zone? I wish I had a clear-cut answer for you; unfortunately I do not. What I can tell you is that fear (as in a warning not to do something that could be dangerous) feels like what you felt whilst doing the Fear Exercise.

Feeling out of your comfort zone generally feels like love with a tinge of excitement/nervous energy. It's like the butterflies you get in your tummy when you have a crush or the adrenaline that floods your system just as you're about to go on stage and perform.

If you can begin to notice these subtle differences in your body as you go about your day, you will be able to better base your choices on love and learn to trust your intuition more. Trust your gut, as is often said.

CHAPTER 5
BE OKAY WITH PISSING PEOPLE OFF

"You've been putting on too many human 'coats.' Other people's opinions are like layers of coats. Stop adding layers upon layers of coats over your own."

The Mothers Club

We've all been faced with situations in which we feel no one understands us or sees the world the way we do. Such lonely times can be scary. Even so, we shouldn't let our fears define our choices. Wouldn't you rather make a decision based on what feels right for you? Even if no one else agrees with you, or offers you validation of your choices? If your life goes pear shaped, at least you will know that you did what you thought best, right?

When we base a decision on what someone else feels is best, we risk blaming that person if things go wrong or praising that person and giving that person credit if things go well. Either way, we have given our power away. From now on, I encourage you to do your best to trust that you know best.

You have access to all the guidance, wisdom, and knowledge you need within you and around you.

Evaluate the facts. Take things on board, and then lovingly ask, "What brings me closer to my joy? What takes me further away from my joy?" Be okay with the idea that, on occasion, your life and choices could piss someone else off—and if they do, that is absolutely okay because you are doing what's right for you.

Do you value what others think of you (or what you *think* they think of you) more than what you think of yourself? If so, how does that make you feel—or as Dr. Phil says, "How is that working for you?" Yes, it's valuable to know how others perceive you, but placing their perceptions above what you know to be true about you is a sure-fire way to take a walk down Disempowerment Street.

Be aware of the opinions of others. Use the ones you value to help you in your personal growth, and leave the rest at the door. People base their opinions of you on the following four filters.

1. Their opinion of themselves.
2. How they view the world.
3. Their upbringings, belief systems, and so forth.

BE OKAY WITH PISSING PEOPLE OFF

4. Their jealousy and insecurities.

So always take what people believe with a grain of salt.

Are you a people pleaser or a people aggravator? Both styles of behaviour are fine, but neither can give you what you really desire, which is most likely more love in your life as well as more joy and peace in your heart.

Pleasers want approval and love. Aggravators want to feel important and have what they say treated as important. They also want to feel approval and love, but go about getting that approval by making what they have to say seem more valid than the things other people say to them. This is aggravating to other people because it can come across as condescending and unpleasant.

Neither way is wrong and neither way is right. But it's great to have the awareness of what you have been doing and why. Which way have you been acting lately? What do you really want? Do you want to feel approval? Do you want to feel love? Do you want to feel like what you have to say matters? Maybe the people in your life are looking for those things, too?

The funny thing about both of those behaviours and objectives is that they are externally driven motivations. Neither has to do with pleasing yourself on your own terms.

IGNITE YOUR JOY

I love the concept of being okay with pissing people off when you make decisions to please yourself. I was a bit taken aback when I first heard about it, however. I was on a cruise ship in the middle of the Indian Ocean enjoying some me-time away from my three-year-old boy (who was in the midst of being potty-trained), and my seasick husband, by attending a lecture given by the talented and inspiring best-selling author Cheryl Richardson. She told the fifty-odd people in the audience that this was the first lesson her own life coach had taught her years earlier and she still found it relevant!

The idea of having permission to piss people off fascinated me then—and still does. You see, many women I know, including me, are people pleasers at times. This means we only do things that we feel are okay with others. Sometimes, in fact, we'll do what's best for others even to our own detriment.

Why on Earth do we do this?

There are a few reasons:

The first reason is that we are modelling the behaviour we saw our mothers, or other primary female caregivers, exhibit. The second reason is that, as women, we are instinctively nurturing and want the people around us to feel loved and cared for.

A third reason is that we want to get approval, as we believe this will make us feel more loved. This last

BE OKAY WITH PISSING PEOPLE OFF

reason is probably one of the biggest reasons we behave this way. Although it isn't something that we necessarily understand on a conscious level, there's usually a little girl inside us pleading, "Look at me. Love me."

The strange thing is that trying to get attention often has the opposite effect of the one we intend.

When we do what is best for us as a general rule, we behave in a much more loving manner toward other people. Sometimes they get angry, but the potential for others to feel disgruntled should not deter us from taking good care of ourselves. This is not to suggest that we should actively choose to piss people off for the sake of it; it's just to say that when we put our own well-being before the needs and wants of others we can feel okay when it happens, because it is inevitable that there will be occasions when it occurs.

So how do you navigate the whole "be okay with pissing people off" concept while at work? Work is such a great training ground for personal development and emotional awareness! You do not want to go about actively pissing off your boss or colleagues. But you do want to recognise what you want that you are not getting from them, and to assert yourself when asking for it, or to be able to say no when you feel things are unfair. The goal here is not to make people mad; it's to find the courage to stand up for yourself. If others get mad while you are calmly and rationally expressing your needs, that's not your responsibility. Be aware that sometimes people use hostility to try to get others to back down or not ask. Don't be intimidated.

In the process of becoming okay with pissing people off, here is some of the really cool stuff that occurs. You'll:

- Find yourself encircled by people who love and respect you.
- Feel more love and respect for yourself.
- Discover that even if you piss people off they still love you.
- Tend to have more honest and meaningful relationships.
- Instinctually invite and inspire others to begin being okay with the whole pissing people off thing, too.

So next time you catch yourself behaving in a way that is benefitting someone else, while detrimental to you, stop it. Stop. It. Then remind yourself, "I am okay with pissing people off." You'll be glad you did.

CHAPTER 6
BE YOUR OWN BEST FRIEND

*"Make it your business to know yourself,
which is the most difficult lesson
in the world."*

Miguel de Cervantes

After working with hundreds of women over the last decade, it still amazes me how horribly cruel we can be to ourselves. When you ask a woman how she thinks she is doing as a mother, wife, daughter, or employer, some of the cruellest ideas come out. And put her in front of a mirror . . . wow . . . what a nasty bitch she can become. In the workplace, women often compare themselves to other women. There can be an unrealistic set of expectations that are set up which inevitably cannot be met and can leave a woman with deep feelings of inadequacy. Add to this a partner and children and things can become even more stressful. Admittedly there are women who have supportive partners, families, and workplaces. However, many do not.

This is where I have noticed many women adopt the "Super Woman Complex." You know the kind I mean, the women who expect to be healthy, beautiful, and financially wealthy, and to have a loving partner, happy and behaved children, and passionate mind-blowing sex. In truth, I just described myself. I do have a belief that I and we can have all of those things, but, as Oprah once said, "Not necessarily at the same time."

Can you imagine if the nasty voice that you have in your own head was an actual person? How long would you keep that friend around for? Not long, right? So why tolerate a nasty inner voice?

One of the greatest gifts we women can give ourselves is the gift of friendship to ourselves. Using something Oprah Winfrey has said she does each time she walks past a mirror, I encourage all of my clients to say, "Hey sweetie," every time they walk past a mirror. This is something that I do myself. This is such an easy, yet powerful exercise that we can do multiple times a day.

Imagine what this could do for your self-esteem.

Louise Hay similarly used to encourage her clients to do mirror work using her affirmations, which are positive statements that describe a desired situation.

BE YOUR OWN BEST FRIEND

A beautiful one to do at work or at home is to look in a mirror and say, "I am a talented and wonderful woman." Louise says she has placed a number of mirrors around her home and office so that she can do her mirror work multiple times a day. This may not be appropriate at your workplace, but it is a great idea nonetheless. Perhaps you can do it in the bathroom during your afternoon break.

> *"You are doing the best you can with the tools you have. When you know better, you will do better!"*
> **—Debbie Zita**

This advice does not mean that you should bullshit yourself (because you'll see right through the lies), just that you should switch your focus from your "faults," which might be anything from how you are not "smart enough," "young enough," or "quick enough" to reach your target or land the promotion you want, to your ability to manage your team, inspire your colleagues, or cook a up a feast for your family and friends.

Mirror work can bring up insecurities about our physical appearance such as an ageing face, wrinkles, or saggy boobs. If you are going to use the mirror to focus and hone in on specific parts of your face and body, try switching it up and focusing instead on the parts that you do like, such as your beautiful eyes, sculpted cheekbones, or your great ass. Seriously, try this. It really does wonders for your self-esteem.

If you are struggling to find even one thing you like about yourself, this is an indicator that you may need some assistance in this area from a professional, as there may be something deeper going on.

We all have things we don't like about ourselves, but that doesn't mean we should be mean or keep our focus on it. After all, would you stand in front of a dear friend and say, "You look like shit today"? Probably not. If you commented on your friend's scraggly appearance, I suspect you'd follow that remark up with, "Honey, you are breastfeeding a newborn and raising three-year old twins! That means you're allowed to look tired. As soon as you can, I know you'll find the time for your appearance again. No matter what, you're beautiful to me."

Doing the simple techniques that I have discussed above can dramatically change the way that you view yourself and the world around you. Having a strong sense of self-worth (which when they're done regularly is what these exercises can give you) transforms the experiences around you.

BE YOUR OWN BEST FRIEND

Let's take for example a woman who is in her late forties who is working as a financial advisor in a firm. She has been there for fifteen years and is aiming for a promotion. She then receives news that not only did she not get the promotion, but that her younger colleague, who is only thirty and has only been with the firm for two years, has received the promotion she wanted. No doubt, this would sting at least a little bit, no matter what type of person you are. However, the woman who is connected to her own worth would look at this set back from a very different perspective than the woman struggling with her own self-worth. For the second woman, this disappointment could be the making or breaking of her.

So I invite you to switch things around, divorce your nasty inner voice, and start saying nice, supportive things to your reflection in the mirror.

If everyone lived this way and understood how powerful positive self-talk was, how much more compassionate might we all be, not only to those around us, but also to ourselves?

Dump Your "Frenemies" and Practice Acceptance

It took me until I was twenty years old before I realised that I could break up with a girlfriend. At that age, it just occurred to me one day that I could say, "Go away!" And when I did, it was one of the most liberating experiences of my life. My former friend was a gorgeous and well-liked individual, but for some reason she had decided it was okay to nit-pick me. So I "divorced" her as an act of self-love.

Seriously, women can be so cruel. If I thought working with my counselling clients brought out the inner bitch in women, I was in for a surprise when I entered the fashion and styling world, where a woman's appearance was the only thing that counted about her. We seem to forget that we are all just learning here, and that everyone else is also here to learn. Understanding that people are doing their best frees us from placing too many expectations on them. This is not to say that we should not expect a certain level of respect and reciprocity. Quite the opposite!

It is important to know that each of us comes with our own unique gifts and view of the world. Sometimes our views do not match up with other people's and thus we may annoy people and they may annoy us. As long as we know that we are doing our best, and they are doing their best, this truth takes away our emotional pressure to try to please people or to get people to act in a specific way to please us.

Try out the idea of accepting people as they are and see if it makes a difference in your life and in the way you interact with your world.

BE YOUR OWN BEST FRIEND

"If you can truly learn to become your own best friend, you are heading in the direction of greatness. Love is the cornerstone for everything in life. Without it you have nothing—or worse, you have fear. Befriend the voice in your head, the face in the mirror. Be kind to her and she will be kind to you."
The Mothers Club

Loving Yourself in Mind, Body, and Spirit

Loving yourself is the cornerstone lesson to igniting joy. This lesson is about self-love: finding it, keeping it, and giving it to yourself. The reason it is so important is that when we are in a space of loving ourselves we energetically create more. We create more networks, more experiences, and therefore more opportunities. Thus expanding our reach and our success is about not only figuring out what our inner joy is but also in executing it.

Love is something most of us know about intellectually, but we're struggling to grasp it emotionally and spiritually.

IGNITE YOUR JOY

This chapter will discuss the concept of love in terms of three main themes.

- **Mind:** Loving your inner child and caring for your emotional self
- **Body:** The art of self-love and caring for your physical self
- **Spirit:** Becoming your own best friend and caring for your spiritual self.

This is especially important when we're uncertain about what we want to do for a living, because we need our strength and a clear mind to explore what it is that we are here to do. When we do not fully understand ourselves in mind, body, and spirit we can miss the signs that are being sent to guide us to know and live our purpose. These may come in the form of specific people or experiences that can lead you to your dream job or to your dream business.

While writing this book, it has been inspiring to see the universe conspire to assist me in my writing process. Many writers would empathize. When you decide to write a book, it's as if you sign yourself up for the learning that's involved so that when it comes time to do each chapter you know what you're talking about. Sometimes this education is a very conscious process and other times it is not.

When I originally wrote the outline for this book, the condition of my mind, body, and spirit (and the care I provided myself, or sometimes failed to provide) was probably that of an average western woman working and raising a family. I would eat three meals a day and drink one or two coffees a day and at least one and a half litres of water. I always tried to eat lots of fruit and veggies. I tried to exercise as often as I could and I would regularly do meditation and saw a counsellor.

Once I completed the outline, I felt utterly exhausted on every single level of my being, so I decided I needed a couple of weeks' break not only from writing, but also from my other business activities. A couple of weeks turned into a couple of months, and a couple of months turned into four months in total. The length of time I took off was not something I had planned, and I often protested it; nevertheless a good, solid rest was what my mind, body, and spirit were screaming out for.

The screams got so loud that I had to listen.

The Mind, Body, Spirit Boot Camp

The four months I took off from writing and doing any form of business became a mind, body, and spirit (MBS) boot camp for me. During this period, I was faced with my most intense fears. I had a choice: face them with love or with fear. I could learn from them and grow, or allow myself to believe that the universe was showing me I wasn't up for the challenge of writing a book, running a business, or managing a household with a young child in it. In the end, you are reading this book now because the choice that I made was love.

It was not easy to get through those four months, often not fun at all. And to be honest, it was occasionally bloody scary! But I was determined to face my lessons with an open heart, and I trusted that the universe would provide me with the tools I needed to help me heal my exhaustion, and use my story as an example so that you may heal your life, too. The mind, body, and spirit are separate entities that work collectively. When one malfunctions, all malfunction.

Welcome to your mind, body, and spirit boot camp. A MBS boot camp is much like providing your car a regular service. It can be costly and irritating when done without a plan or professional support, but with the right mechanic and the right tools it is well worth the effort. By the end, you feel better than new.

Mind: Loving Your Inner Child and Caring for Your Emotional Self

The emotional relationship we have with ourselves begins in childhood, as do the patterns of how we relate to others do. The cradle of the family is where our emotional learning takes place. In order to become emotionally healthy as adults, we must know how to connect with our inner children and learn to respond to their unmet emotional needs. This all sounds very simple, of course, but when you are living and learning it may be challenging to meet the unmet needs of your inner child. Let's break down the process, therefore, into the lessons that I was faced with during my own boot camp. These will be followed by simple exercises to help you on your journey.

Lesson: Trust Your Journey

When you are intimately connected with your emotional self, you begin not only to trust yourself, but also to trust the events and the people around you.

In saying "to trust others," I want to be clear that you should not be foolish or ignorant in regard to putting your faith in those around you. Some people have not healed their own wounds and may not want the best for you. When they do not, your discernment can show you how to maintain boundaries that protect you from harm. This may be keeping your plans close to your heart so that you can write that business plan or book without the interference of other people who may be jealous of your drive and success.

IGNITE YOUR JOY

What I mean by trust is trusting that the people who have entered your life are here to show you something about yourself that you need to learn and will grow from learning.

Who showed up in my life to help teach me to trust my journey?

The Universe's Teaching Method: Rejection

Oh, my dear friend rejection, we have laughed and cried together (mostly cried). You have shown yourself to me in the face of past lovers who did not want my love, past employers who were not in need of my talents and services, and the girls at school who didn't want anything to do with me. Just when I thought our friendship had finally said its last goodbye, you showed up again with that look in your eyes, and before I knew it I was back in your arms.

We are all faced with rejection. It sucks. It feels like crap. But it is a necessary part of our evolution. Coping with rejection assists us to strengthen our mental, emotional, and spiritual muscles in the process. Imagine what your life would be like if you'd never been rejected—ever!

I know there are a blessed few who can say, "Every guy I've ever liked has liked me" or "Every job I have applied to, I have gotten," but for most of us this isn't the case. If you're like most people, and like me, then you have faced rejection.

Rejection can be as simple as smiling to someone on a train who does not return that smile. It might be attempting to change a lane while driving and not being able to get in because none of the other drivers will allow it. Simply put, rejection is part of the human condition.

What did I learn from my own experiences of rejection?

The Outcome: I Am Enough

Once in a while, big rejections occur and hurt my feelings, in the process reminding me of prior rejections. These memories for me go as far back as early childhood. At eight, I was frequently teased at school and I felt tremendously rejected by my classmates because of it. In 1999, my first boyfriend, a guy I loved dearly, left me and moved on to his next relationship only a month later. After that, my self-esteem plummeted and my inner dialogue sounded like this: "Everything I try fails. Not only am I not smart enough, I am not lovable enough either!"

At university, I learned psychological techniques from the study of cognitive behavioural therapy (CBT) to deal with healing these sorts of psychological patterns. From my personal experience, I can report that these do work—but only for a short time. Once you are hit with another big rejection, the patterns can come back again unless you do something more to address your feelings. There is a better way to overcome negative patterns and take them as lessons, which is to engage the universe in teaching you. It's a means to interrupt the inner dialogue.

Let's go back for a moment to the thought, "I'm not smart enough, not lovable enough." When this thought arises in my head, it's as if I am directly requesting to have these qualities and experiences from the universe. It's almost as if I am saying, "Please send me people and experiences that prove that I am not smart enough and not lovable enough."

The universe replies: "Okay, if that's what you are asking for. Here is what you ordered . . . a cancelled client, a rejected application to a university course, a fight with a close girlfriend, an unhappy husband."

In response to any of these outcomes, I might then say to myself, "See, I was right. I am not smart enough and I am not lovable enough either." Then the cycle of manifestation would go on and on until something or someone broke the cycle.

I am blessed to have access to wise and loving support, both in the physical and the spiritual worlds.

BE YOUR OWN BEST FRIEND

"Imagine running a marathon without the right training? You could hurt yourself doing that. That is why you have trainers. That is why you work hard and learn all the things that you need so that you can run that marathon to the best of your ability. We want you to do things to the best of your ability as well so that you can get the most out of them. And whether or not you win first place in the marathon is not important either. It's the fact that you ran it. Now stop being childish and start recognizing that you are more than enough."

The Mothers Club

From the spiritual world, I can get an energetic slap across the face and a hug at the same time when I get dejected. My inner knowing says, "What on Earth are you doing? So, a few things did not go according to your plan. You think that means you are not smart enough, not lovable enough? No! It doesn't actually mean that at all. It only means that now is not the right time. It means you are not ready, and you have more work to do. We love you and want the best for you, and we are here helping you along the way so that you can have a happy life, a contented family, and live your life's purpose.

IGNITE YOUR JOY

The gentle, spiritual slap across the face really is a beautiful thing. This is not only available to me, but to everyone who is willing to ask for help. The key to receiving messages and support from the spiritual world is to have gratitude for the things that you do have, and to be open to the love and support that the universe wants to provide to you. That love and support sometimes show up in unexpected ways.

Think of the bank manager who wakes up in the morning with the flu and has to call in sick, later to find out that the bank was robbed that day. Possibly in that moment the bank manager feels disappointed or upset, not realising how the day will unfold.

In learning to trust the journey and go with the flow of life during my four-month hiatus from working, I allowed myself to have space to learn and to grow. The result was that I became a better version of myself at the end of those four months.

The Mind Exercise

As I mentioned, I am an advocate of CBT, so I have devised an exercise that incorporates CBT in combination with affirmations. CBT aims to help uncover and alter distortions of thought or perception in order to change negative behaviour and emotional states. Here is an example.

BE YOUR OWN BEST FRIEND

Problem: A woman is having difficulties with her boss who often ignores her at work.

Step 1: Ask yourself what does that mean to you? In this example, the woman asks, "What does it mean to me if my boss ignores me?"

Her inner dialogue might be, "My boss always ignores me. He does not like me or my work," thinking that means, "He must think I am incapable " The result of this type of thinking is that every time her boss ignores her, in her mind she hears, "I am incapable and not good enough ."

Step 2: The next step is to challenge the painful thought and look for evidence of its truth in reality. What is the supposed evidence that the woman's boss thinks that she is incapable and not good enough? In this woman's mind, it's that he "ignores me." But in looking for this evidence of her boss's actions and possible feelings toward her, she also realises, "He is happy when I have monthly meetings with him. He says encouraging things like, 'Well done,' when I sign a new client. Therefore, maybe there is no real evidence that I am incapable and not good enough."

IGNITE YOUR JOY

Step 3: Replace the original thought whenever it comes up with an alternative thought that you feel to be true. In the case of the woman in our example, this could be a thought such as: "My boss does think I am capable and good enough, he might just be stressed and overworked."

Please note: In this scenario, this boss might or might not believe this woman is capable and good enough. The point here is that the woman has been letting her thoughts dictate her feelings. Until now, if her boss ignored her, she felt incapable and not good enough. Her boss's behaviour and possible rudeness was reminding her that she felt incapable and not good enough. By using CBT she can "catch" the thought that's upsetting her and replace it with a more productive one.

Another tool that I like to use, as mentioned previously, is the affirmation. These are repeated many times in order to make an imprint on the subconscious mind and trigger it into taking positive action. Affirmations are a way we can program the mind in the same way that a computer can be programed.

Let's use the same example. We know that this woman feels incapable and not good enough in her boss's eyes. The more that she focuses on that premise, the more she will start to behave like someone who is incapable and not good enough. In order to help her create a work life where she feels capable and good enough, it is important for her to affirm, "I am capable" and "I am good enough." These wonderful affirmations are a way she can reprogram her subconscious mind.

When first affirming something, it can feel foolish. But once it becomes a daily ritual, it really is amazing what can be achieved. I am an advocate of Louise L. Hay's work with affirmations, and so I would do as Hay recommends in her books and take the process a step further with the instruction that the affirmations be done in front of the mirror at least three times a day for a minimum of seven days (as mentioned previously).

Body: The Art of Self-love and Taking Care of Your Physical Self

Self-care involves truly listening to the body's needs and providing it with the care and love that it is asking for. This means being conscious about the foods we eat and the exercise and rest we provide for our bodies, as well as the clothing and accessories that we adorn our physical temples with. It is about recognising that your beautiful, perfect body—no matter what shape, size, or colour it is—is yours. It should be treated as your masterpiece.

You are like an artist and your body is the canvas. Connecting to that part of you is a wonderful way to express yourself authentically.

IGNITE YOUR JOY

In 2012, Australians collectively spent a staggering AUD$6.99 billion on beauty products, an increase of 18.8 percent from the year before.[1] In the United States in the same year, the revenue of the cosmetic industry was $56.63 billion.[2] Similarly, at retail in 2010 in the European Union revenues of the cosmetic industry came to EUR€67 billion.[3] We spend our money expecting to fall deeper in love with the reflection we see in the mirror. But is that working? Have we truly begun to fall deeper and deeper in love with that reflection or have we just noticed more flaws?

Buying more stuff for your body when you don't have adequate self-care is like plucking your chin hairs; just when you think you got them all you notice another one and another one. It's useless. And why is it that we always notice them just before an important meeting when we are in the car and don't have any tweezers! *Grrrrrrr.*

The truth of the matter is that we all have flaws. Yes, even you. Yes, me. And yes, even that "perfect" supermodel on the front cover of the magazine. If we're all flawed, why are we so concerned that ours are worse than anyone else's? We spend so much time waxing and plucking, primping and tinting, adding this and subtracting that, cutting off fat here to put it there, whitening, straightening, curling, bleaching, gelling . . .

And for some people, that's just what they do before lunchtime!

BE YOUR OWN BEST FRIEND

Why do we do all of this? Because we so desperately want to feel happy. Unfortunately, it is exhausting—and it is not working. We're not feeling better, so there is clearly something wrong. Could it be that we are looking for our happiness and self-esteem in the wrong places?

In terms of joy, caring for the physical body is a very important aspect of a working life. Notice how many millions of dollars have been spent on makeover shows and exercise shows. We have become quite obsessed with witnessing those transformations. Why? Because maybe it gives us a feeling that we do have some control over the partners we attract, the jobs we attract and the opportunities we attract.

Lesson: Your Body Is Your Temple

When we are able to honour and respect the premise that our bodies are temples, we shift our whole beings into alignment with the universe.

Being spiritually oriented, it's easy for me to become disconnected from my body. I know that this is the case for many highly sensitive individuals, such as mediums and others in the field of spiritual transformation. Quite frankly, sometimes being in the body is not as much as fun as being out of the body. The spiritual realm can be filled with such amazing insight, love, and connectedness and such an awe-inspiring sense of higher consciousness that coming back down to earth after being in trance or having an out-of-body experience can feel like a chore. But what happens when we spend too much time out of the body? We become unbalanced, confused, and disconnected from ourselves and others.

In order for us to live authentic lives, we must keep the mind, body, and spirit in harmony.

The Universe's Teaching Method: Physical Exhaustion

The first half of 2012 was a roller coaster. I had enrolled in pretty much every transformational workshop, business seminar, and writing conference I could physically slot into my calendar. I had forgotten the rule that just because you can neatly fit a ton of appointments into your diary doesn't mean that your body (or your mind and spirit) can cope with that amount of activity. Being the Sagittarian that I am, however, I set out to prove to myself that I could. I told myself that I could write a book, run a business, and raise a son all by the end of the year! Truth be told, I could have. What, in my excitement, I forgot to do was maintain my balance in the process.

What started out as excitement and joy in my body quickly began to resemble Groundhog Day. The alarm would go off in the morning and my heartbeat would escalate immediately. I would have a quick look at my smartphone before I even left my bed,

BE YOUR OWN BEST FRIEND

planning, *Okay, email him, ring her, make lunch for my son, text my new client, contact the tech guy* . . . In the process I was shocking my body with adrenaline in order to have enough energy just to start the day.

Once a met deadline had come and gone, then my body was allowed to rest. My defenses were down and this allowed me to understand, at last, what my body needed and was telling me. What I felt was sheer and utter exhaustion. I planned to take off a couple of weeks, which became a month, and then turned into four months.

During this period of rest and recuperation, I booked a session with a kinesiologist. Kinesiology is an alternative and holistic therapy involving the study of movement. The belief is that by using muscle monitoring, a practitioner can identify imbalances in the body that may be causing health problems. My kinesiologist, Sharon Tal, advised me that my adrenal glands were out of whack (a non-technical term). She pointed out that because I had been in a pattern of go, go, go, rest, go, go, go, rest, my body was screaming for some balance. I knew she was right. Having always felt that my life was a sprint instead of a marathon I'd been through rest phases many times before. I wanted a more permanent solution. "What's the solution?" I foolishly asked.

My kinesiologist put the instructions for a detox diet (an anti-candida diet to be exact) in front of me and asked me to follow the plan for twenty-one days. On this plan, I had to eliminate refined sugar (although I was still allowed to eat one apple, one small banana, and one grapefruit per day) and caffeine. This was a diet that I'd been shown at least five times in the past either by a naturopath, a general practitioner, or a friend. This time, I decided that enough was enough and I had to do it.

If you've ever come off sugar and caffeine, you'll believe me when I say that this commitment was one of the most challenging things I've ever done in my life—and I include losing my mother and giving birth among them. For the first seventy-two hours, I felt ill. I was more exhausted than before. I was in a constant state of nauseousness. I had headaches, felt dizzy, and experienced intense cravings for sugar. I mean *intense*, as if I would have *killed* for sugar. I felt like an addict coming down from a high. Approximately forty-eight hours into the detox, I realised that I had two weddings and two hen nights coming up. But I had come too far to start again later. I was determined to do this without going back.

Once I got through the severe first seventy-two hours, I noticed something miraculous occurring. Because I had not given in to my cravings, I allowed myself to connect to what was really happening in my body on all levels. One day I woke up craving chocolate milk. My craving was so intense that I rang my kinesiologist and asked her permission, "Please, can I have milk? Chocolate milk is not so bad."

BE YOUR OWN BEST FRIEND

She said, "Darling, you can have what you want, but if you want to shift from up-and-down energy to stable energy, you will need to follow this plan exactly for twenty-one days at least. Now tell me, what is going on? Why the craving for sweet milk?"

At first, I was confused. "I just want it," I told her.

She wanted to know *why* I wanted it. What did the milk represent to me?

I was silent for a minute as I considered her question, and then all of a sudden I burst out crying. "My mum," I told her. "I miss my mum. I miss knowing that there is someone here who comforts me, who nurtures me, who supports me the way only my mum could. That's what chocolate milk means to me." As soon as I said this, the craving was gone and I got reacquainted with my old friend grief.

Confronting the cause of any problem (which for me was my grief) is not an easy thing to do. For this reason, I recommend that you have a solid support network around you when undergoing any kind of detox. Once you can reconnect with the root problem, you are on the way to shifting from a place of victimisation (also known as fear) to a place of acceptance (love).

IGNITE YOUR JOY

The Outcome: Balance

During my detox I began having an intimate connection with my body. I began to recognise when I was starting to feel stress. I began to recognise when it was time to stop and rest. I also began to connect to the brilliance of the mind, body, spirit relationship. I began to live my own life in balance.

Ultimately I ended up continuing the detox until I reached day 23 (a special number for me) and somehow, through many miracles and with much self-determination, I managed to attend those two weddings and two hen nights on my calendar.

After the twenty-three days of detox, I did not return to my old ways. I simply did not want to. As a result, I now have an organic, decaffeinated coffee approximately twice a week. I eat much less meat. My diet predominantly consists of organic fruit and vegetables and good proteins, like legumes and wild salmon.

My diet may not be in line with anyone else's ethics or body, but it does not have to be. All of us have to discover for ourselves what works for us. This way of eating works for me. The massive reduction of sugar and caffeine especially has allowed my body to naturally find its own energy level so I do not have the awful comedowns that I once did. I also feel calm when I hear my alarm ringing in morning.

BE YOUR OWN BEST FRIEND

After over thirty years, I am now finally finding my own rhythm and really enjoying my body. I have lost some of the baby weight from when my son was born, which is a nice thing, too.

The Body Exercise

Our bodies are a miraculous tool for self-discovery, once we allow ourselves to attune to them. Have you noticed that when you cut yourself you have the intuitive knowledge to look after the wound? You might wipe it with antibacterial solution and put a Band-Aid on it, or if there is a lot of bleeding you might decide to go to the doctor or hospital for stitches. As it begins to heal, you know to take off the Band-Aid at rest time to allow the wound to breathe. This is knowledge that you may have picked up from a first aid course or by watching your parents or teachers.

It's easy to recognise cuts and bruises when they physically manifest on our bodies. It can be a bit challenging to do this when they manifest inside our bodies. During my detox, I was privileged enough to partake in a weekly workshop known as the Art of Feminine Presence. Participants spent three hours every week over ten weeks learning a number of practices. One of my favourites of these is called Tune In and Check In. We would start every session with it.

IGNITE YOUR JOY

Here are the instructions.

1. Get comfortable, either in a seat or on the floor, and then close your eyes.

2. Breathe very deeply in and out at least three times. I prefer breathing in through the nose and out through the mouth. As you do this, imagine breathing in love, peace, and positive energy. As you breathe out, imagine breathing out stress, negativity, and anything toxic.

3. Next, ask: "What are you feeling physically, emotionally, and energetically?" Start by really tuning in to it in great detail.

4. Ask: "What are you feeling physically?" Start from the top of your head and scan every part of your body all the way to your toes. Is your physical body relaxed? Maybe it's tired, sore, or tight? You do not need to do anything other than to just notice.

5. Ask: "What are you feeling emotionally?" Are you happy, sad, confused, or exhausted? Again no need to do anything. Just observe. This is just about becoming aware.

6. Ask: "What are you feeling energetically, or spiritually?" Are you feeling expansive and loving? Maybe restricted and afraid? Again, just notice.

7. Once you are aware of what you are feeling on all three of these levels, you can then ask yourself: "Where is this coming from?" There is no need to go too much into a story; just become aware

of your feelings. As an example, doing this exercise I might discover that physically I am tired, emotionally I am sad, and energetically I feel flat. The thought that pops into my mind could be a silly argument I had with my husband the night before. I might then realise that something that I thought I had processed and shifted through is still lingering in my being.

8. Ask yourself: "What is this really about?" In my example, let's say it's because I am holding onto the thought that I am unlovable.

9. Once you know this thought (whatever it is for you), you are aware. There is nothing else to do other than to accept your feelings and allow yourself to feel them.

Sometimes becoming aware and accepting what's going on for us in the moment is all we need to do to process and shift things.

Soul: Taking Care of Your Spiritual Self

Once we've begun to master the care of our physical body and emotions, we can connect to a deeper place of inner guidance and wisdom. True love must begin with the self. The spiritual promise we make in honour of living the best lives we can is about connecting with your life purpose and your joy. Given that we spend so many hours at work, it is important that this time is spent doing something that you enjoy which connects you deeply to your soul.

IGNITE YOUR JOY

Lesson: Love Is All Around You

We spoke a lot about love versus fear in Chapter 4. If you've been walking a spiritual path for a while, this idea that love and fear go hand in hand is probably not new to you. In my experience, love and fear are also related to the soul and the ego. The ego fears, whereas the soul loves.

The Universe's Teaching Method: Abandonment

Many of us suffer from the fear of being alone or abandoned. In many cases, this is why we choose to date, love, and commit the rest of our lives to people who may not be treating us in the most loving ways. It's almost as if we feel that the crumbs they are throwing our way are better than nothing at all.

A couple of years ago, I was introduced to a lovely client named Cassie. Her name has been changed to protect her privacy. Cassie had lost her mother nine months prior and begun an affair soon afterwards. In her thirties and married with three children, Cassie came to see me after discovering my website online.

Like so many women, Cassie had spent her life looking for love. She'd had many relationships that began well and soon became dysfunctional and quickly ended. Cassie thought she had found true and lasting love with her husband, but after discussing their marriage with her, I soon discovered that their marriage was not at all what it appeared to be on the surface. Cassie told me that they had not been sexually intimate for five years and that she had been having an affair with a work colleague for the previous six months.

After the death of her mother, her husband had been far from supportive. Cassie felt shattered and that she and her husband had tried everything to mend their bond. When she met her now boyfriend (a man who was also married with children), she felt desirable and loved for the first time in many years.

Over the next six months, Cassie and I worked together to empower her to discover what it was that she truly wanted for her life and how she could go about getting it. Eventually, she told me that she was madly in love with her boyfriend. Even though she was unsure that he felt the same way, she could not stand living a lie anymore. Cassie was absolutely terrified of confronting her husband, but decided to do so once she discovered that, like her, he was having an affair. Once the cat was out of the bag, Cassie's husband left their family home.

Cassie felt devastated that her husband was also having an affair. This was not something she was expecting. But she admitted she also felt free for the first time in many years.

Cassie soon ceased her sessions. Three months later, I got a call from her saying, "My boyfriend left me. He said he can't handle my insecurities and wants a four-week break." Her worst nightmare had come true. First her husband had left her for another woman, and now her boyfriend had, too. Cassie was broken hearted. As we worked together over the next twenty-eight days to mend the pieces of her shattered heart what happened was nothing short of miraculous.

I devised a twenty-eight-day soul detox plan for Cassie. (It appears at the end of this chapter in the exercise section.) Please note the length of time: twenty-eight days. This is a similar length of time that it would take to complete a drug and alcohol rehabilitation program. Like drugs and alcohol, lack of self-love is an addiction and can be scary and very challenging to overcome.

The Outcome: Self-Love

The journey to self-love can be one of the most challenging experiences in the world. It is a time for you to intimately get to know yourself. For many people, the first step is to make a commitment to want more and have more. This is usually referenced directly to our romantic lives, as that is where our version of love plays out. After enough heartaches a person (in many instances) says, "Enough is enough! I want more." That is a great start, but unless she has support and defines practical tasks, wanting more can become nothing more than just a meaningless concept.

BE YOUR OWN BEST FRIEND

In Cassie's case, she not only wanted more, she also was willing and prepared to put in the hard work necessary to get her version of "more." Cassie found this time extremely confronting and at times terrifying. She very quickly was able to recognise when she was falling into bad habits and she would turn to her support network (and the tasks I set her) to assist these overwhelming feelings.

So what happened at the end of the twenty-eight days? I know you are on the edge of your seat wanting to find out. Cassie's boyfriend did not make contact. Cassie herself did, as she wanted to "know where she stood." By week four, Cassie had blossomed into a vision of strength and realised that the relationship she had with her boyfriend was not something she wanted again. She still loved him, but by now she realised that it was hurting her to stay engaged in their dynamic.

She spent the last week of her soul detox focusing her energy on loving herself, getting emotionally strong, and writing a list of non-negotiable qualities that she wanted in her next relationship (whether with this man or someone else). She was hopeful her boyfriend would accommodate her, but she was also a realist and was prepared for him not to.

When Cassie met with her boyfriend, despite being instantly physically attracted to him she was also energetically repelled. He looked "gorgeous," but according to Cassie, "He has not grown emotionally at all." He offered her the chance to pick up where they had left off, and Cassie respectfully declined.

Cassie like so many women is a beautiful looking, highly intelligent, and emotionally loving human being, yet she had not been recognising those qualities within herself. Therefore, she was attempting to find them outside of herself. Through all of the hard work that she did, she began to see herself the way I and many others see her. When she finally caught a glimpse of the reflection, she realised that the person she now saw in the mirror deserved so much more than what this particular man was able to offer her.

Her focus began to shift from romance to her family, her purpose, and her career. Cassie is currently content with life and working on unlocking her life purpose through different career opportunities. She would love a partner and is open and receptive to a respectful, loving relationship when it happens, but by stopping the constant focus on her romantic life she's actually able to concentrate on finding her authentic life purpose and enjoying her work and just being herself.

BE YOUR OWN BEST FRIEND

The Spiritual Detox: Twenty-eight Days to Love

I invite you to do the same type of spiritual detox that Cassie did. You may begin immediately if you wish to, or choose a start date in the future and spend at least a couple of days preparing. Each week of the four-week spiritual detox has different goals. Do your best to stay on the step you are on. Below you will see a list of instructions.

Week One: Soul Searching

This week is all about allowing yourself to feel. It is important that you do not skip this process, as it will only be more challenging to deal with your feelings later. We can try and bury them with a fling, a big night out, or eating a bucket of chocolate ice cream. At the end of the day, however, any buried emotions will resurface. Now is the time to deal with them head on.

In preparation for this week, stock the house with loads of fresh fruit and veggies, and try and have some meals frozen ahead of time, or even better cooked for you by someone else. You might be feeling very emotional and drained, so cooking might not be the last thing on your mind. Next, enlist the love and support of very close family and friends. An ideal number to think about is five friends. They will be like a hand of support, and each is a finger. Your support system is absolutely vital, because you will need them during this time.

IGNITE YOUR JOY

An example of five supporters could be:

1. Your best friend,
2. Your brother or sister,
3. Your mum or dad,
4. A counsellor or psychologist, and
5. Your family doctor.

I realise for some people finding five members for a support network could be a challenge. Some other places of support to include might be your local church or place of worship, and Lifeline or the Samaritans (free telephone counselling services available 24/7). The key here is to enlist people who you feel have your absolute best interest at heart and are willing to commit to your well-being.

Activities during Week One

During Week One, do the following activities.

- Keep a daily journal. Use a prompt for your writing, such as: "Dear Me, I am feeling . . ." Or: "Why does this keep happening to me?" Then keep writing.

- Write a letter/journal to your past lover or past lovers.

- Write a letter to your current or past boss (anytime where you felt undervalued or unappreciated).

- Check in with yourself twice daily, in the morning and at night.

- Use the Tune In and Check In exercise from page 98.

- Do a minimum of twenty minutes of exercise every day (even just taking a stroll). This is absolutely necessary, as exercise releases a chemical called serotonin, the "happy chemical." Exercise will assist you in recovery by getting any pent-up frustration and anger out of your system.

- Create a list of nurturing things to do (see the instructions in Chapter 4 on how to devise a Stress Prevention Plan). Look at this list every time you need TLC.

Week Two: Realisations

This week will be filled with aha moments. Keep your journal on hand to write down anything that comes to you. You will most likely begin to see connections and themes that have emerged in your most recent relationships and in past relationships. This includes personal and professional. It may feel like a game of connect the dots.

I want to add here that although the aim of this book is to explore your joy and purpose at work, there are so many wonderful lessons and insights hidden within our romantic and familial relationships. So please do take note of these, too. Existing within them are golden nuggets and keys of valuable information.

Remember, we are all different, thus you will go through your recovery at your own pace. For some people, Week Two may feel better and easier than Week One did, while for others (this is not uncommon) it may feel even more challenging. We all know the saying, "Ignorance is bliss." These realisations may not always be pretty to look at, but you can only change what you are willing to acknowledge and accept.

Activities for Week Two

During Week Two, do the following activities.

- Write in your journal every day about what realisations have surfaced and about what has triggered something in you emotionally. For example, notice what irritated you.

- Create your own personalised affirmation booklet. You will need to purchase a mini-notebook, something that has a pretty colour or image on the front that resonates with you. This is to contain your own personalised affirmations and must be kept on you at all times. Start by adding three affirmations on the first day, and then a minimum of two more every day until your notebook is filled with goodness. Be sure to write one affirmation per page in big writing.

BE YOUR OWN BEST FRIEND

Here are some wonderful examples:

> "My work is joyful."
> "I experience joy effortlessly."
> "My life is filled with joyful people."
> "I trust the process of life."
> "I trust myself."
> "My mind, body, and spirit are in perfect harmony."

An affirmation is your assertion that something you wish to exist already exists. For example, if you want more money, you would affirm, "I am financially abundant.." If you want a great job, you would affirm, "I have a job that I love." I recommend you focus your first ten to twenty affirmations on Joy and then branch out to cover other areas of life, such as Love, Career, Finance, Family, Health, and Mother Earth.

- Read at least three affirmations out loud twice a day (morning and night) while looking into a mirror.

- Once your booklet is complete, use it as an oracle guide. By this I mean, turn to a random page to find the affirmation that your intuition has chosen for you on a particular day.

IGNITE YOUR JOY

- Create an affirmation journal. Using another notebook (so now you have three journals in total), spend every day this week journaling what comes up for you as you read the affirmation. Do this by looking deep into your eyes as you repeat the words and then becoming aware of the reactions your mind, body, and soul are having.

  > What is your mind doing? Is it telling you that those words are a lie?

  > What is your body doing? Is it resisting (tightening)?

  > What does your soul say? Let it uplift and inspire you.

Write everything down and start a conversation with your mind, body, and soul. A great example is this: "My work is joyful."

The mind says, "No, it is not."

The body says, "My chest feels tight and I can feel my sore back."

The soul says, "This experience is bringing you closer to understanding who you really are."

The key here is to recognise the thoughts and feelings that come up and start talking to them.

BE YOUR OWN BEST FRIEND

Remember that the mind is ruled by ego, so it is constantly comparing and doubting, looking for places to fault you. The body tends to mirror the mind. If an anxious thought pops up, the body will tighten. The soul, however, is pure love and only wants the best for you and everyone. That is the best voice to listen to.

This is a learning process so be patient with yourself, and remember that you really are loved.

Hearing the voice of the soul can take time and practice.

Week Three: The Purge

This week is about detoxing. It is a time to release the old and make space for new energy to enter your life. It is not a time to wish bad or hate anyone. On the contrary, it's a time to thank all people and circumstances for entering your life. It is through these people and experiences that you have learned and grown, so this is all about being grateful for that opportunity as you let go and move forward. This is something you can do in your mind or in writing if you feel to.

IGNITE YOUR JOY

Activities for Week Three

During Week Three, there are only two activities to do.

1. Write a letter to the person who is causing you the most pain right now. This might be an old coworker, boss, friend, or lover. This ritual will assist your releasing process. It is a guide only. Begin it with: "Dear old . . ."

2. Write a collective letter to anybody else who you believe to be causing pain. Fill it with any feelings that come up for you. They may be angry, they may be hurtful, and that is okay. This is about letting out any toxic emotions that have been living inside of you so that you are ready to embrace the opportunities that are coming your way. Often the feelings are quite similar: for instance, feelings of not being good enough (rejection) or feelings of being misunderstood or not fully seen or heard.

Once you feel that your letters are complete, it is time to burn them. Please do this outside in a safe area where you can contain the flame in a non-flammable container. As you watch the flames in the air, please imagine all of the energy that it contains being picked up and taken away by a beautiful golden light. If you are someone who is connected to angels, fairies, spirit guides, or ascended masters, you may wish to visualise these beings of light instead. This light, in any form it appears to you, will transform this dark energy into love and light and send it back to you and these lovers for healing.

During or after the burning process, please thank all those who hurt you and forgive them. Remember this does not mean that you condone their actions; it means that you forgive these people. Thank them because within the hurt you felt is the lesson of self-love. They have provided you with the opportunity to spiritually evolve and truly love yourself.

Week Four: The Declaration

This week is all about moving forward with love and gratitude. It is about accepting the experiences that led you to this journey of self-love. It is a time to truly live in the now and trust the timing of your journey.

Activities for Week Four

During Week Four, there is only one activity to do. Write a declaration letter. This is a lovely ritual that is designed to skyrocket you into the hemisphere of love. It is about forgiving yourself for any wrongdoings that your ego has led you to believe to be. It is a ritual of healing. Write these exact words:

Dear me, myself, and I,

I am sorry for any hurt I caused you. I want you to know that I am here for you now and always.

IGNITE YOUR JOY

I love you and will continue to love you no matter what happens. No matter what others do to you or you may to do others knowingly or unknowingly, I love you unconditionally.

All my love,
Me, myself, and I

Please sign and date this letter and keep it in the drawer of your bedside table or near you.

Now you are ready to step into life with a feeling of lightness, trust, and ease. Take the time to write a plan now of what it is that you truly want for your life. Some questions you could ask yourself to assist this process are:

- If I could wave a magic wand, what would my life look like?

- If I had a genie that could effortlessly place me in the perfect job and life, what would that look like?

- If I had all the time and money in the world, how would I spend my time?

- If I had all the money in the world, what would I do for myself, my family, and the world?

CHAPTER 7
TRANSPARENT SISTERHOOD

"Nurture your body, stop competing with others, and befriend your inner child."

The Mothers' Club

We are in this life together, so it's essential to find someone you trust with whom you can share your joys and sorrows. If you cannot discuss the things you are going through with your sisters, then who else can you share with? On the journey of you, developing strong social support outside the workplace is going to enable you to be more effective in the workplace, to be more creative and inspired, because you're more than a machine that works, works, works; you're flesh and blood with feelings.

Over the years I have met many women who have amazing and inspiring stories to share. In fact, I truly believe that inside everyone there is a book or a movie script just waiting to be written. As Mark Twain said, "Why *shouldn't* truth be stranger than fiction?"[1] I understand that not every woman is comfortable sharing her experiences (not even with her closest friends). It depends on her personality and upbringing. However, I have noticed that some amazing things take place when a woman dares to be vulnerable and actually shares her deepest most vulnerable parts with another.

Here's an example. Many of my girlfriends have experienced miscarriages or post-natal depression. Since I've always been known as the resident counsellor and healer, it is not uncommon for my friends, or even strangers, to share intimate details with me and declare, "No one else knows this." I began to notice that a few people I knew (who also knew each other) had gone through similar experiences. So I approached two women separately and asked if they minded if I shared a part of their story with a woman going through a similar experience, as I believed it would comfort her. Both women said yes and even said, "Please tell her to call me." Once I disclosed to each woman who the other was, both were comforted and surprised.

I was honoured to facilitate and open up a dialogue for these women, and then I began to question what it was that kept them silent. Being an extrovert and an "over-sharer" by nature, I found this baffling. As I began to investigate by questioning women around me, what I discovered was this:

- Some women felt ashamed and embarrassed.
- Some women did not want the emotional responsibility of rehashing painful experiences.
- Some women did not want to be labelled as having been through cancer, depression, low libido, and so on.

It also became apparent that every woman I spoke to was happy to share her story or experience on almost any topic if she felt it was going to benefit another woman on her journey of coping with something similar.

Women are natural communicators and nurturers. When I refer to amazing things happening when we share, I am referring, for example, to witnessing a woman breaking down in front of a group of women in a safe and sacred space as she speaks openly about her deep sadness and grief. What is so beautiful is that in that moment that woman is helping her healing journey by letting go and feeling safe to share and usually what follows is at least one other woman who breaks down declaring that she had been through a similar journey and was so comforted to know that she was not alone. This last part provides further healing for both the woman who shared and the woman who listened as they recognise the strength within each other and the power to help heal another woman. This powerful exercise often creates beautiful events, such as lifelong friendships, the setting up of support groups, businesses, and or projects that raise awareness on a certain topic.

The concept of transparent sisterhood is powerful and necessary. If we look at ancient cultures, it would be unheard of to go through any emotional or spiritual trauma without the support of your tribe. Furthermore, for anyone who has been on the spiritual path for a while, you will be familiar with the concept of the rise of the feminine. This is not to say that women must rule (although if you asked me that would not be such a bad thing), it is however, about the rise of feminine energy versus masculine energy, leading to the restoration of balance.

Feminine energy may be described as one of inclusion, nurturing, and lifting the group up as a whole. Masculine energy may be described as seeking domination. This has little to do with individual men and women, as within each and every one of us both feminine and masculine energy exist. Both energy paradigms hold negative and positive qualities. It is critical for them to balance one another.

If you are lacking relationships with nurturing and compassionate women, maybe it's time to join a meditation group, a goddess circle, or another such group with a focus that appeals to you. There are usually plenty to join. Hiking anyone? Or create your own group. The members could be entrepreneurial women from the same industry as yours, or just people who share your same leisure time interests.

TRANSPARENT SISTERHOOD

You might align yourself with women who are going through the same experiences as you in their personal lives. If so many of us are suffering from post-natal depression and miscarriages, or are coping with infidelity, shouldn't we be talking with our trusted girlfriends about these experiences? If we are not, we are denying ourselves the experience of welcoming someone else into our world. We are also missing out on the rewards of offering a helping hand to another woman who is going through a similar issue as ours, but is too afraid or ashamed to discuss it. The more of us who begin speaking to one another from the space of authenticity, the more we can truly support each other and trust that we are being supported.

Discovering and Befriending Your Shadow Side

You are perfectly imperfect. Do you know your shadow side? Do you know the intimate details of the you that you try to hide from the world? The you who swears in front of her kids. The you who slept with that guy during your business trip to Asia last year. The you who can't look at her own reflection in the mirror. The you who lies to herself that it's only a couple of glasses of red wine, when in reality she's been drinking an entire bottle of wine by herself every Friday night for the past eighteen months. The you who regrets getting pregnant at a young age. The you who can way too easily finish off an entire tub of ice cream without even slightly feeling full.

IGNITE YOUR JOY

There is a reason why we women love characters like Bridget Jones and Carrie Bradshaw. They represent the parts of us that we are not comfortable exploring or admitting exist. They give us the sense that someone is at least as messed up as we are, if not more so. For a moment, when we watch their escapades and how they make fools of themselves on TV or in a movie, we feel better about our flawed selves.

Bridget Jones represents a full-figured woman with the worst luck with men. No matter what she does, she seems to constantly land flat on her face. The charming thing about her character is that she ends up finding what she wants: a loving husband who adores her for who she actually is. Women all over the world adore this character and identify with her because she is so charmingly imperfect.

But what happened to the character of Bridget at the end of the last frame of the movies, when the director yelled, "Cut. It's a wrap." What happened to the character that we all grew to adore and cheer for? Did Bridget live happily ever after? Did she have two and a half children and a house with a white picket fence? Or did life throw her one too many curveballs? If she was like the women I know and love, she continued making mistakes even as she lived happily ever after. Real life has its ups and downs. We do as best we can with what we know to do. But it requires us to be honest about our strengths and weaknesses.

TRANSPARENT SISTERHOOD

Acknowledge Your Weaknesses

In order to get to know the diamond that you could be, you must be willing to embrace the chunk of coal that life is moulding into shape. How can you expect the world, and those in it, to love parts of you that you yourself hate and reject?

This is not to say that you should like every part of yourself, but it does help to acknowledge your weaknesses and either a) accept them as part of you, or b) work on overcoming them.

When you give yourself permission to shine, you inspire others to do the same. Part of the process of shining is allowing your light to dim periodically. After three months of winter, we thoroughly appreciate the beauty and warmth of the summer sun. Likewise, after you allow yourself the space and courage that it takes simply to be with your darkness, to just sit within the uncomfortable for a period of time, then magic happens. You begin to know yourself on a deep, intimate level. And that's when you begin to notice the opportunities around you and have the courage and strength to step into them.

Sitting in silence with your thoughts and feelings can leave you breathless, even paralysed, with fear during a moment of darkness. But if you do sit still, without distraction, this is where healing takes place. This is where transformation takes place. This is where you can encourage yourself to go a little deeper, feel a little more, cry a little harder. There is such beauty held within that darkness.

When you emerge from the cave of your inner darkness, you emerge as a different version of you. A brighter light. You are not without fault, but you are accepting of it, and possibly on your way to creating a new character trait, or a new version of you, whose beauty can be thoroughly appreciated by you and others.

Acknowledge Your Strengths

Once you have sat in a place of emotional discomfort and gotten to know your flaws, it's time to step out and spread those wings of yours. This is the cocoon-to-butterfly stage. There is something beautiful about coming to this point in time. Not only do you have a deep appreciation for it, but somehow more authenticity exists when you have confronted your fears and said, "Okay, I see you."

This liberating experience is not only beneficial for you but also for those around you: friends, relatives, colleagues, clients, and customers. There is a particular energy about a person who has walked through a dark tunnel and found the light at the other end. In the words of Marianne Williamson (this is my all-time favourite quote):

TRANSPARENT SISTERHOOD

Our deepest fear is not that we are inadequate. Our deepest fear is that we are powerful beyond measure. It is our light, not our darkness, that most frightens us. We ask ourselves, who am I to be brilliant, gorgeous, talented, fabulous? Actually, who are you not to be? You are a child of God. Your playing small does not serve the world. There's nothing enlightened about shrinking so that other people won't feel insecure around you. We are all meant to shine as children do. We were born to make manifest the glory of God that is within us. It's not just in some of us; it's in everyone. And as we let our own light shine, we unconsciously give other people permission to do the same. As we are liberated from our own fear, our presence automatically liberates others.[2]

PART III
YOUR LIFE PURPOSE

The concept of life purpose has become popular in mainstream spiritual culture. Purpose has become yet another commodity for us to try somehow to attain, almost as if by figuring out and living a purpose we will discover the secret to life and joy. Clarity of purpose certainly does assist us in experiencing more joy in our lives. However, being purposeful is a journey not a destination. The chapters that follow are intended to assist you on your journey to understand your purpose and become aware that everything you are and do is part of your life purpose.

CHAPTER 8
SING YOUR SONG

"A bird doesn't sing because it has an answer, it sings because it has a song."

Maya Angelou

"To be living 'on purpose' is to be living a life that is conscious. A life that is fully awake. Any 'on purpose' pursuit will involve being of service. Everyone's life purpose (in other words, your reason for being here) is different. Just like a grain of sand or a snowflake, no two are exactly the same. 'Being of service' is defined as 'assisting the life of another in order that they may feel nourished and nurtured.'

"Why do this? So that they may reach a point of inner strength and empowerment and eventually move on to assist others. You are of service to others so that one day THEY may be able to be of service too . . . and so it continues."

The Mothers Club

IGNITE YOUR JOY

After working extensively in the area of life purpose over the last three years, I have developed an equation to make finding your purpose as easy as possible.

Timing + Talent + Skill = Life Purpose

What Is Timing?

Your life purpose moves through three phases:

Phase 1: Preparation. Here you accumulate lesson after lesson (like badges of honour).

Phase 2: Integration. This stage often feels a bit boring or "blah." You may have the feeling that there has got to be more to life.

Phase 3: Application. You are blissfully happy and work does not feel like work. Ideas flow, money comes effortlessly, and things seem to spontaneously fall into place (or at least there is a strong trust that they will).

It is important to note that once you move through these three phases, the process starts again. Do not be surprised if after living in flow for a while, you find yourself back in the preparation phase.

Can we speed up the process? Yes!

How?

SING YOUR SONG

With:

- Acceptance.
- Finding peace within the chaos.
- Mind-body-spirit awareness.
- Adopting a nonjudgmental attitude.

These approaches will help you to move and process the energy of your purpose a lot faster, improving your timing. Sometimes by trying we actually tamper with our productive energy. Just by *being*, more healing occurs on an energetic, and a practical, level.

What Is a Talent?

A talent is something that comes naturally and is a joy. Something you love to do.

What do you love? Although you may have been told doing something particular is a "waste of time," usually your life purpose will involve something that you are naturally talented or gifted at. So if you hear this comment, feel free to ignore it!

What Is a Skill?

The ability to do something well (expertly).

How do we learn skills and become expert? Through pursuing the *themes* in our lives that teach us lessons.

IGNITE YOUR JOY

I'm so grateful for every single experience that I've been through in my life up until this point: the good, the bad, and the awful. Why? Because I would not be who I am today without having had all those experiences and learned from them. They taught me lessons that helped me build my skills.

What do your experiences have to do with finding your soul's life purpose? Your experiences are always shaping you and preparing you to live and practice your soul purpose. I love it when people say they are attending the University of Life, because that honestly is what life is. It's as if you applied to the perfect classes and are doing the perfect major with the perfect teachers and assignments to educate, train, and otherwise prepare you for your industry. It's quite magical actually—at least in hindsight.

Much like attending university (from my experience anyway), life can be stressful, exhausting, and even incredibly boring at times. But when you realise you have completed your assignments and earned your certificate, there is a feeling of huge accomplishment. Then, and oftentimes without realising you have enrolled, you move on to getting your bachelor's degree, your honours, maybe a master's degree, and if you are really good, a doctorate.

Here's an example to help you.

SING YOUR SONG

Case Study for Sharon

Timing Stage:
Integration–Application

Talent: Love of people, friendly environment, cafe life
Skills: Good with money, good judge of character, good in business

Sharon's life purpose = Creating spaces for women to "nurture, empower, and grow."

So now we know that we learn these "skills" via the themes in our lives that teach us LESSONS.

A Tool for Finding Purpose: Evaluating Your Life Themes

Themes in life are only valuable if you use them to truly learn something about your character. What themes have repeatedly shown up in your life thus far? Looking back on repetitive experiences, what have they taught you about yourself and others?

Have you noticed some patterns emerging in your life? For instance, do you seem to attract disrespectful or challenging partners in love? Maybe you keep having issues with housing or safety? Or maybe you keep changing jobs, careers, or courses, constantly feeling unsatisfied? You may have experienced all the above, so pay particular attention to the one or maybe two recurrent themes that really piss you off or give you the feeling of having been thrown off course.

It can be difficult to notice thematic events before they happen, or even as they are happening, but in the wonderful light of hindsight you'll begin to notice some familiar scenes popping up again and again and again. It's almost as if you are an actor playing a part in a movie. The scene has a different name and the characters are slightly different, otherwise it is pretty much the same scene being replayed multiple times.

Once you are in a place where you feel grounded and open, sit down and meditate on the topic of life themes. Do your best to remain emotionally detached and begin to replay various scenes in your mind as if you are simply watching someone else in a movie. Some topics to get you thinking are:

- Romantic love
- Family
- Housing
- Health
- Work
- Money

A few points to remember:

- If you have access to your soul's past-life experiences and you feel that these are linked

to your current lifetime, take note of their themes, too.
- Many people have a number of different soul purposes, so this exercise can be repeated annually or whenever you feel that your life is moving in a new direction.

Noticing a theme that is negative, such as the theme of loss/grief, does not necessarily mean you will constantly struggle with this topic throughout the remainder of your life. The lessons you have already learned in relation to that theme are what matters. Furthermore, noticing how a theme has affected you can give you insights about clearing and healing any residual negative energy you may still be holding on to. Once lessons are integrated, you will move on with a newfound awareness and a lighter energy surrounding that situation. Think of this process as layers of an onion being peeled back. It may never leave your system completely, but you become highly aware of it and it becomes an extra in your life rather than the starring role.

You Are Closest to Your Soul Self at Birth

If you gaze upon the wonder that is a newborn child, it is hard not to believe in miracles and a place beyond this earthly realm. Even the biggest of sceptics can look at a baby and wonder, *Where have you come from?* The answer in its simplest form is God (or Universal Consciousness/Higher Power/True

IGNITE YOUR JOY

Source). That beautiful child of God has come from a place of love and light and is here on Earth ready to grow, learn, and teach the lessons of its soul.

With this in mind, I believe it is necessary to revisit your inner child as a way to connect to a time of wonder and curiosity that often becomes squashed and diminished as we grow older. We take on the roles and responsibilities bestowed upon us by our family, religion, community, and the world at large.

The idea of revisiting your inner child has two benefits: first, a lot of healing can take place in the process. Second, it connects you to that part of you who remembers who he or she is before he or she was asked to forget; this is the part of you that remembers who you are spiritually, not just humanly. I must add here that it can be an emotional journey to revisit this part of your life, particularly if you had some sort of trauma as a child. Therefore, it is recommended to employ the help of a professional.

A child is born perfect, without self-consciousness or affectation. If you sit and watch children playing, you'll see that they're in the moment and entirely unaware of what others are thinking. If they want to roll in the mud, they roll in the mud. If they feel like eating sand, they eat sand. Though their choices may not always be the wisest, they are experiencing life at a deeply meaningful level.

SING YOUR SONG

Children are experiencing life in a state of never-ending optimistic wisdom (NOW).

Oftentimes, as we grow up, we become concerned with expectations placed upon us. We become conditioned by the commonplace. Expectations come from our family, schools, churches, and other places of worship, and the media. We are fed information every moment of every day. There simply is no escaping this fact. Every time we turn on the TV, read the paper, or just look outside our windows, our senses are being inundated with information that tells us how we supposedly should look, feel, eat, sleep, work, play, and smell, and even how we should have sex. During this process our inner light dims.

Why do we try to adapt ourselves to social opinion? Simply put, humans are pack animals and it is in our nature to do what the herd is doing. It is a survival tactic. We want to feel loved, connected, and appreciated, so we do pretty much whatever needs to be done in order to either gain or maintain status. For a short time, this process works. Feelings of love, connectedness, and appreciation are wonderful while they are occurring, and this makes us happy.

If you ask anybody what they really want out of life, the answer, nine times out of ten, will be happiness. Our happiness often seems to be tied up in various packages, such as a new partner (love), a new job (status), and more money (success). Although at the end of the day, happiness actually comes from another, deeper source that exists inside us, the reason we want those things is that we believe they will make us happy.

Sounds good, doesn't it? But if you are reading this now, it is because somewhere inside that beautiful heart of yours, you know that what you and I and everyone else are really seeking is that something deeper. It still might be called happiness, but it's really a particular kind of happiness: the kind that makes your heart sing with joy, the kind that isn't dependent on the day of the week, the time of the year, your pay cheque, or marital status. This kind of happiness is everlasting because it is connected to your soul.

"How can I achieve this kind of happiness? I hear you asking. The answer is: by remembering why you are here and by living your soul's life purpose.

It is often said that we regret the things we don't do more than the things we do. Living life fearlessly and "singing your song," like a bird would naturally sing, is about leaving your mark on the world while your soul still has access to your physical body. Your journey of you is to follow the soul's path, to sing the soul's song.

Let's use the example of a woman who loves to cook: She is happiest when spending time in the kitchen because this is where she is at peace, at one with herself and the universe. In this example, her "song" might be baking cakes. She may not have realized yet that her soul adores baking. But as she gets to know herself better and her soul begins to "sing," she realises her song is her love of food and the joy it brings to others.

It is important to dedicate ourselves to doing what we love so that we may share our joy with others on a regular basis. This is not about starting a business. It is about living our bliss. For the food lover, other examples of what she could do to share her love include writing a cookbook, starting a cooking school, or simply donating time and skill cooking food for people at a shelter. This act is about creating a deep connection with ourselves and expressing our gifts while we have time and a body to do so.

> "When you leave your physical body, it is not uncommon to miss it for a while. So while you have it, use it. It is perfect. It is yours. No one else on Earth has a body and gifts quite like yours. Let them shine so you can become a beacon of light for others to do the same."
>
> **The Mothers' Club**

IGNITE YOUR JOY

How I Discovered My Life Purpose

I believe there are some blessed individuals who were born knowing what it is that they were meant to do. My beautiful mother adored children and for the twenty years of her life before she started a family, she was a primary school teacher. For her that was absolute bliss. She loved watching the children in her class learn and play. She worked in an impoverished area with children who often came to school feeling sad and scared. Being the person that she was, she would lavish them with kisses and cuddles, and made sure they left her class room with smiles on their faces and joy in their hearts. I believe this made her feel needed and important.

It was not as simple for me to find my life purpose. I love doing a lot of things and I'm good at a lot of things, too. This is lovely, of course. But though you might assume that being good at lots of things would make it easier to choose my path, it actually made things more difficult for me. You see, I used to think that being good at something meant I would like doing it. Like my mother, I adore children, so after completing high school I enrolled in an early childhood studies program that would qualify me to teach kindergarten. Everything was going well. I enjoyed learning about childhood development. I was even getting straight A's (something I usually had to work very hard for, as I never found being "book smart" easy).

SING YOUR SONG

Wonderful, I thought. *Everything is going according to plan.* That was, until I had to complete my one-month practicum at a child care centre. Oh boy, was I caught by surprise! Teaching kindergarten wasn't for me.

Being good at something isn't the same thing as pursuing your soul purpose. Your soul purpose has to do with something that makes you feel joyful and inspired. While in theory I loved the idea of being a kindergarten teacher, once I'd tested out the experience, it was blatantly obvious that I was studying for the wrong career.

After the practicum, I transferred to the psychology department to earn a bachelor's degree in behavioural science. I had a dream of becoming a child psychologist; however, I felt way out of my depth in the course and struggled for three solid years. By giving it my sustained, absolutely best effort, I scraped through. Since I did not receive the marks needed to get into the honours year that would follow my undergraduate work, I spent my summer vacation trying to figure out what to do next. I felt gutted: rejected, scared, and confused.

Next, I enrolled in a program that would bring me a bachelor's degree in social work. I could have gone for a master's degree in counselling, but my ego got in the way. By this I mean that in truth all I ever wanted to be was a counsellor but I felt it more important to belong to what I thought was a more prestigious profession. The masters of counselling was taught by psychologists so I was annoyed that I was not one of them, hence I chose social work instead. Although social work never really suited me, I figured that being a social worker would put me in what I thought would be a more regulated industry. I wanted to feel like I belonged. I completed my second degree in 2005 and once again found myself at placement hating every single second of the job I was doing. Those three months honestly felt like three years.

By that time, I was twenty-four and desperately wanted to move out of my mother's home and have some independence. I also wanted to marry my boyfriend. I stuck out doing social work and ended up getting a job in outreach, aged care mental health, meaning assisting mentally unwell elderly in their home I lasted eighteen months in this position. During that time, I broke up with my boyfriend and met someone new, the man who would become my husband. My wedding came and went with all the usual stresses you would imagine. I had been married for only four months when I was diagnosed with clinical depression. My condition was not bad enough to be hospitalised, but I definitely needed a break. So I quit my job, applied for a pension, and took three months off.

It's strange how things turn out sometimes. I don't like to regret anything that has occurred in my life, as I believe even the most difficult experiences have a higher purpose. That purpose is to teach us more about ourselves so we may grow into wiser, more

SING YOUR SONG

loving human beings. But I have always wondered whether my life would have been different if I had gone after a master's degree in counselling. In hindsight, counselling seems more in alignment with who I am now as a person and the way in which I work with my clients. Still, I see it as a moot point. My sense is that I would have ended up basically where I am now. I would likely have reached the same destination by walking a slightly different path.

After my episode with depression, I really had to dig deep. I was scraping the bottom of the barrel personally and professionally. Anything had to be better than where I was at that point. In the process of looking within, I learned to forgive myself for being what I thought was "weak" and I began to map out a life for myself that would bring more peace and joy into my life and the lives of those around me. Once I felt stable, I went back to a profession I had been involved in while I was attending university: ladies' fashion retail. I have always been really good at selling and I adore fashion, as it helps women to feel good about themselves. At this juncture, I also set up my own online business selling accessories, designer clothing, and gifts.

Things were going beautifully. I was working hard and for the first time felt happy to go to work every day. I had to tell my ego to take a hike because it kept insisting that something was not right about spending six years at university, at a cost of over $30,000 dollars, only to end up selling ladies' fashion. But I was happy and I decided this was more important than what my ego thought about my job.

During this joyful time of forward movement, I became pregnant and life seemed blissful (except for my extreme morning, afternoon, and evening sickness). Of course, my bliss was short lived because my mother was diagnosed with advanced liver cancer just as I reached my second trimester. As you know, she passed away a mere eighteen days after receiving the diagnosis.

After my mother's death, nothing really made sense to me anymore. What I had been working towards seemed to dissolve. I stopped working in retail, dropped my online store, and went about the business of trying to prepare for the birth of my son while mourning the death of my mother. That became my job.

I took myself to therapy, both doing one-on-one counselling and participating in mother-loss groups. I was determined to bring a healthy baby boy into the world and be a happy and stable mother for him. I tried my absolute hardest to soothe myself emotionally (and did a pretty great job of it, too), but I still ended up experiencing severe post-natal depression. It was a condition I had desperately been trying to avoid given my history. My son was eleven months old, and this time I was taken to a psychiatric hospital for treatment. Once again, I found myself at the bottom of that bloody barrel. I needed, sought, and received professional help to climb out.

I can recall the second night at hospital. The doctors had sent my son home so that I could get a proper night's sleep for the first time since his birth. I was pacing the halls with discomfort because I was still breastfeeding my son at that stage and my breasts were swollen with milk. I remember saying to myself, *This feels pretty much as bad as it gets. Mum is dead, I'm in the loony bin, and now I'm weaning my son off the boob from the loony bin.*

I spent a total of four weeks in hospital. Once I was out, I began the process of rebuilding my life yet again.

Can you see some patterns emerging for me? Work hard/burn out is one. Pushing through and doing what I feel I have to, another. Then there are other themes, such as depression and loss and grief. It took me a while to notice this for myself, but I truly believe that the universe was sending me a message. The universe sends us messages to try and set us on the path of our soul's purpose. The universe starts by tossing a pebble at us, then a rock, and then a whole house lands on us. It does whatever it takes to get our attention until we get the message.

What lessons did the themes in my life teach me about myself and others? For many years, one of the themes in my life was romantic love that was unrequited or ended in heartbreak. I had my first crush, which lasted three years, starting at age six. My second crush was "love" at first sight at the ripe age of nine, and this time the feeling lasted over two decades. That boy gave me my first kiss and then I spent about fifteen years experiencing feelings of inadequacy, as my love was not reciprocated by him. That was just the fun beginning of the theme of romantic love derailing and upsetting me. During my late teens to mid-twenties this theme emerged again. This time it involved one of my best male friends, who pursued me for six months before coming out as gay three months after I finally started dating him. That does not do wonders for a gal's self-esteem.

Then there was my first real romance, which was an on again-off again affair that occurred between the age of sixteen and nineteen. It ended with my heart being broken, and then broken again, repeatedly, because I was forced to watch him date. Did I mention he was my sister-in-law's brother? For this reason, I couldn't avoid being around him.

Three years after that relationship ended, I was set up with my ex's cousin. Yes, that's right; I dated both my sister-in-law's brother and her first cousin. In fact, I even attended my first love's wedding with his cousin.

Surely that would be enough for me? No. I would become heartbroken again. After eighteen months of dating the cousin who was not ready to commit— or at least not to me—we broke it off, and between the cousins I dated my dentist's son for two and a half years.

Wow, I'm exhausted just writing about this string of relationships. But I hope it's helping you form a picture of how themes work? Clearly my heartbreak was a theme that kept popping up. Once I identified that, I realised how this theme could offer me awareness and insight that can benefit me in all areas of my life. I believe everything we experience is a tool for us to grow.

Want to know how the relationship theme ended? I did finally meet my Mr. Right.

How did I meet Mr. Right? One of my closest girlfriends had ended a long relationship with him just five months prior to my breakup with my first love's cousin. According to her, he was devastated and needed a friend. She was moving to South America for over a year and decided that since I was heartbroken and a good listener I might be a good friend to him.

Suspecting her reasoning might be faulty, I made her ponder the wisdom of introducing me to her former boyfriend for a whole week because, first, I had decided I never wanted to talk to another man again, and second, what if—bizarrely—a real romance developed between us?

My girlfriend rang me the day prior to her departure

and assured me, "I would be really happy if it did." Well, it did and she was not.

Mr. Right and I started out as friends for the first four weeks, speaking every day. Our connection was so powerful that eight weeks later we were engaged. My husband and I have now been married since March 2006 and have a beautiful son together. My girlfriend could not deal with the situation, so she and I did not speak again until my mother's sudden death in 2008. I was beyond emotional when I saw her at Mum's funeral: I was ecstatic that we were able to reconnect.

So what did all of this romantic drama and experience teach me?

- To love myself
- To be honest with myself
- Always to have respect for myself and others
- That just because someone does not love you the way you love them, does not mean they don't love you the best way they can

Everything we do teaches us lessons that we can incorporate in many areas of our lives. Although I learned to love myself and be honest with myself in the context of my romantic life, these skills ultimately helped me pursue my life purpose. Romance was a proving ground for skills that also apply in business.

SING YOUR SONG

They inform my professional partnerships and interactions with clients and vendors.

Your Talents Can Help You Identify Your Purpose

What are you best at? What do you love to do: dance, sing, paint, or talk? The medium through which your life purpose is expressed will always be something that is pleasant and fun for you to do. Remember, it is not only what you are good at; it also makes you feel great. Another clue that lets you know you are on the path of your life purpose is that people love you when you are doing it—whatever it is.

Expressing your talent could require you to develop a certain level of self-confidence and trust in yourself because you may have been teased for "wasting time" on this talent as a youngster. Maybe you loved painting or music, but your parents said, "Go do your homework instead." Now, even if such voices are stuck in your subconscious mind, if you cultivate your confidence, you can respond to them objectively.

Possibly your talent is to inspire large audiences as a speaker. Such people, and I am one, are often told, "You talk too much," when they are kids—and sometimes as adults, too. The trick is to begin to recognise comments past and present that were and are criticisms of you when you're pursuing your talents, and view them as little reminders of what makes you special. They are gifts and beautiful blessings for you and your world. It's important to forgive the people that make these types of comments, and thank them for being little messengers about your soul's intended work. Now, for instance, if my husband says, "You talk too much," if I'm in a serious mood I respond, "Thank you. Yes, I do talk a lot, as that is how I get my message across," or if I'm in a funny mood, I just say, "That's how I roll!"

How Will You Know If You Are Living Your Soul Purpose?

You know that you are living your soul purpose if you are blissfully happy. Your work does not seem like work. You have constant ideas flowing. Money comes to you effortlessly. Things fall into place. If they do not yet, trust that this is simply part of your journey.

How do you know if you are on track to living your soul's purpose? You accumulate lesson after lesson after lesson. Think of these lessons as your badges of honour. You are accumulating medals for your very own hall of fame. Your soul purpose must be a big one, so hang in there! The world needs you.

SING YOUR SONG

"When you are living your bliss you radiate joy, and when you radiate joy you raise the vibration of the energy within and around you. This joy is contagious and infectious. All who come in contact with you are moved by you and want to find their own joy.

Can you imagine a world filled with people living their joy? Imagine how that would affect everything from the oceans to the earth to the animals. Humans would feel wonderful and would not need to medicate with drugs and food. This is the answer to world peace!

Live your joy. Love yourself and other people. That's why you're on Earth!"

The Mothers' Club

CHAPTER 9
ACCEPTANCE

"Life runs in cycles. The wheel never stops turning. No matter how dark the night, morning comes. No matter how cold the winter, spring comes. When you feel despair, know that the wheel is turning. Joy will come."

Susan Santucci

One of the most important lessons to learn on the journey of you is acceptance of self. This is something that I see people struggling with on a daily basis. Sometimes it seems as if everyone, from my clients, to my friends and family, are griping about not accepting themselves enough. Self-criticism is a trap that's easy to fall into.

IGNITE YOUR JOY

Self-Acceptance

Acceptance follows becoming your own best friend, as it involves embracing all parts of you. I want to introduce a new aspect to this message, however, which is to accept your thoughts and feelings.

Are you confused? On the one hand I am asking you to change your thoughts so that you are "speaking" to yourself in a more positive way. Now I'm asking you to accept negative remarks. *Well, Debbie, which one is it?*

It is both. You see, I am a firm believer that changing your thoughts begins with accepting what you are already affirming—even if it's a negative thought.

If, on a daily basis, you are telling yourself, "I have fat thighs," and then switching gears by affirming, "I have sexy legs," the affirmation will probably sound and feel like complete BS. To your subconscious mind, it will seem as if you are trying to play a trick on yourself.

I know from experience that tricking yourself only works for a short while. Sooner or later those "fat thighs" will come back to "bite you on the arse," so to speak. What I suggest instead is to adopt a more believable approach. Simply acknowledge that you believe you have fat thighs and accept this fact. Affirm, "Yes, okay, maybe I do . . . So what?"

ACCEPTANCE

So what is a very powerful attitude!

This is not to deny that it's a good idea to exercise and eat right. But in that moment of saying, "I have fat thighs," obvious BS would only serve to make you feel awful.

Another thought that may accompany "I have fat thighs" is "and therefore I am unattractive." We reach a point where, in this case, the four words I - HAVE- FAT- THIGHS can send us on an emotional roller-coaster ride of negative thoughts and emotions. Those words ultimately lead us to conclude, "I am unlovable."

You may or may not be conscious of having the belief that you are not worthy, but I can all but guarantee you that if you dig deeper and deeper, that is the negative affirmation underlying any self-image issues you've got cropping up.

Straight away, please accept that you are perfect exactly as you are right now. See that any thought that pops into your mind is just that: a thought. If you are diligent, with practice you'll develop the ability to recognise derogatory thoughts and stop them in their tracks by saying, "I accept that I think or feel this way about myself. Thank you, thought (or feeling) for visiting me; I do not need you to stay."

IGNITE YOUR JOY

Acceptance of Life

"Though no one can go back and make a brand-new start, anyone can start from now and make a brand-new ending."

Carl Bard

Life is ever changing. Just like the seasons, nothing in life stays the same for long. As a result, we need to learn how to cope with change, which can feel like loss. Coping with loss in itself can feel like a merry-go-round ride. As you know, I lost my mother quite suddenly when I was four months pregnant, and I recall that after that loss my emotions went up and down, up and down, as my mind spun around and around. The birth of my son was a bittersweet time. On the one hand, I brought a healthy, beautiful baby home. On the other, I was mourning a death.

Change can often feel like a death in our lives. We can get so attached to our friends, partners, jobs, and possessions that when they are gone we feel bereaved. The truth, of course, is that we all go through changes in our lives, so we must come to terms with impermanence and transitions.

In order to release the kinds of fears that surround change, we must learn to live in the now.

People often go about their lives and relationships exactly as their parents did; or else they make a

ACCEPTANCE

point to do the opposite (so as not to repeat the mistakes of the past). I have noticed a pattern that my current clients share with my past clients (back when I was working as a social worker.) Once they're aware of how their unresourceful behaviour has been influenced by their family of origin, they are freed to choose new behaviours that enable them to attract and maintain more positive friendships and harmonious, loving relationships.

> "I may be up here, but I am not Godly. I may have acted imperfectly, but I am perfect. You do not need to carry any fear that I passed on to you. I never wanted that for you. I lived the best way that I knew how to at the time. You do not need to carry my burdens. The best thing that you can do is to live your most amazing life, the one you dreamt of as a child. The one I saw in your eyes when you played. Show me that spark again. While you are a soul in a human costume you can play any part. Cast yourself wisely, beautiful. Cast yourself wisely."

The Mothers' Club

IGNITE YOUR JOY

Spiritual Practices to Help You with Acceptance

It can be very challenging to accept the things that happen to and around us. I may be challenging some of your beliefs about fate or why bad things can happen, but I really do believe that everything happens for a reason. One of the ways I came to terms with the death of mum at a time when I felt I needed her the most, was to find that place within me that believed or even knew (I say "knew" because it is a knowingness) that everything I have been through in my life has assisted in shaping me into the woman I am today.

"He kissed my stretch marks," said the legendary Shirley Valentine in the hilarious movie by the same name. (This was one of my mum's favourite movies. She used to declare, "You will understand when you are older," and indeed, she was right.) There is a wonderful scene where, after sleeping with a Greek sailor, he comments to Shirley that she should appreciate her stretch marks. "They show that you are alive, that you have given life; don't be ashamed of these marks. They are beautiful."

The realms of spirit are dimensions that hold a perspective about life and death which is beyond comprehension to our human selves. Tapping into these realms can offer you insights and truth about the beautiful impermanence of your life. I find such beauty, wisdom, and love in them. I visit when I need to connect with my truth. It's so beautiful to be in

ACCEPTANCE

the spiritual realms that sometimes I find it a bit of a challenge to return to my physical body. It is very important to recognise this and do grounding activities that can help bring you back. Such activities may include walking on grass and eating veggies or nuts (anything harvested from the soil), or simply visualising the roots of a tree going from your torso through your legs and feet and going into Mother Earth.

Exercise 1: Higher Self-Connection Meditation

Done correctly, this meditation can fill you with a sense of your authentic power and confidence, bringing you greater inner peace and calm as a result. Set aside half an hour to an hour to accomplish it. It has five phases. All of the phases are interconnected parts of a single, flowing visualization that will occur while your eyes are closed. You will need to read the instructions carefully before entering into the meditation so that you do not have to interrupt it in the middle.

Repeat this meditation whenever you feel the desire for a higher perspective.

Preparation: Space Clearing and Archangel Michael Invocation

Before you begin, it's essential to clear the energy in your meditation space and create an ideal ambiance so that you'll be safe and spiritually protected.

IGNITE YOUR JOY

Smudge the room with the smoke of a burning bundle of sage grass (you can purchase this at any new age store). By this I mean, light a bundle of sage or burn a small piece of sage in a non-flammable metal bowl, and then circulate the smoke throughout the space with the intention to cleanse it. You can wave a hand to circulate the smoke or fan it gently with a feather. Be careful not to stir up any embers.

Smudging is a practice that eliminates old, stale energy or negative energy. After you're done, play your favourite calming music and light a candle or an oil burner. You can also burn a stick of incense or ring chimes. All of these things will raise the vibration in the room.

You can also use my favorite spray, Energy Clearing, made by Infinite U.

Next, using your own words, call upon Archangel Michael and ask him to protect you and the space from negative energy during your meditation period. A simple invitation ("Archangel Michael, please protect me") is sufficient.

Optional: You may place a crystal, such as selenite, at your feet or directly in front of you on the ground. This is a great tool to pull out any negative energy that you might want to get rid of. Please be sure to correctly clean and program the crystal by placing it in direct sunlight or the light of a full moon, or putting it under running water or candlelight (not in the

ACCEPTANCE

candle light but just above it). You can program it simply by placing an intention on it before each use, such as "to clear the energy field and protect me." Please "clean" your crystal after each use.

Optional: You may rub a drop of massage oil on your third eye, the spot in the middle of your forehead located directly between your physical eyes. This will assist you in opening your third eye chakra to higher spiritual energy and intuitive wisdom. *Caution: Only use oil that is safe for contact with the skin. Do not use heated oil from your oil burner or undiluted essential oils, which could sting you.*

Once you are comfortable and ready, you may begin.

Phase 1: Journey Through the Garden

Close your eyes and find yourself standing in the middle of a beautiful garden. This may be likened to a garden you've physically visited or it may be an entirely new place. If you are not a visual person, connect to the feeling of the garden, and to the sound and the scents of the garden.

I suggest that you mentally place some gorgeous trees, flowers, and water features in the garden. Place a swing, birds, or children playing in it. Imagine flowers in every array of colour giving off divine scents. Imagine it is springtime and you can feel a lovely breeze and sunlight gently warming your skin.

IGNITE YOUR JOY

Staying in the garden, take three big, slow, deep breaths in through your nose. Then release the air out through your mouth equally slowly. Imagine yourself becoming calmer with each deep inhalation. See yourself releasing the stress of the day with every full exhalation.

Once you feel really present in your beautiful garden, turn around and walk along its outskirts until you find a door. You may notice that the door is smaller than usual or that it's covered with plants. It almost feels like a secret garden door. Stand in front of that door for a moment. When you are ready, open it and walk through.

Behind the door see a staircase leading to a hallway. Go up the stairs and enter the hallway. This area feels very secluded. At the end of the hallway you will see a big door. This door is very special, as it's the entrance to a divine place: the home of your higher self.

The door you find may be ornate. You may see guards standing in front of it or security tape around it. Some people see a lock or a voice-recognition box outside the door. That's because this place is just for you to enter and no one else. If anyone else is ever present in this space it will only be because you have invited them to be there with you.

Use the key that you find in your pocket, speak the necessary password, or open the security tape as necessary to open the door. Then, open the door

ACCEPTANCE

quickly and step inside the sacred space, ensuring the door is locked behind you. Inside this room you should have a feeling of complete peace and security, a feeling of coming home. This is your space.

Walk around the space and familiarize yourself with your surroundings. There might be flower arrangements, a spa bath, or a lovely chaise longue in the room. There may be nothing adorning the area at all. Perhaps your space is a crystal cave with light beaming into it from every angle. There is no right or wrong. The space is whatever it is for you.

Phase 2: Your "Home" Office

Scan the room until you locate a desk. This is your office space, a place where knowledge and information is stored. When you see it, please sit down at your desk. Then notice if there is a laptop on it, or a pen and a pad of paper. You may find a written note on the desk waiting to be read by you or else you'll be guided to write something yourself. If so, read or write.

If you feel stuck or simply would like to gain more insights, ask questions, such as:

- Why am I here?
- What guidance can you offer me?
- Is the circumstance I am currently in here to teach me something? If so, what is it?

- Is this person (be specific) someone I need in my life? Why or why not?
- What is my life mission or life purpose?
- Am I a healer or some sort of spiritual teacher?
- What steps do I need to take in order to move forward?

If you aren't seeing, feeling, or hearing much of anything, that's okay. It can take practice to access the wisdom of the higher self. Consider your visualization a learning process. At least now you know where your higher self lives, and how to go and visit at any time. On the other hand, if information is coming, but it is coming at you too fast or too slow, please feel free to telepathically ask for the flow of information to slow down or speed up.

Once this process feels complete, please thank your higher self for the information.

You are now ready to move on to the next phase.

Phase 3: Mirror, Mirror on the Wall

Scan the room until you see a big mirror. Leave the desk and go stand in front of it.

Many of us find this part of the journey to the realms of the higher self a bit daunting, because the mirror in this space is just like our mirror at home: We don't

ACCEPTANCE

always like what we see in it. But this is a necessary part of the process if we want to move forward in our lives.

When you feel ready, please take a look at your reflection in the mirror. What do you see? Is it the physical you? Is it a younger or older version of you? Whichever version of yourself you see, look deeply into your eyes in the mirror.

As you stand in front of the mirror you may be shown images or scenes, like in a movie. Most often images and scenes are from a past life. If they begin to show you imagery, you may ask that only that which you need to see be shown—and for it to be shown in an emotionally neutral way (in other words, without disturbing details).

If information comes up that's encouraging, please take note of its guidance and wisdom. If anything comes up here that is of a negative nature, I want you to stop and ask yourself:

- Why do you think that?
- Where did that come from?
- What steps can I take to release myself from this?

Find out what lesson needed to be learned in the past-life or imagery you're seeing. Ask for guidance in removing any energetic remnants of that life or other past lives which may be linked to your current life. When you do you may be shown tools that you can use to release negativity.

If you need specific guidance, try the following:

1. Imagine the source of any negativity as a physical wound on your body. Then see a stream of white and golden light penetrating the wound. Watch in the mirror as the wound disappears.

2. Imagine placing any fears that are associated with a negative trait into a box. Ask Archangel Michael to take it to the light to be restored and healed. Watch in the mirror as the box is carried away.

3. Imagine yourself wrapped up in chains. Then see an older version of yourself and a younger version of yourself cutting the chains with pliers. Ready? Do it on the count of three: 1 – 2 – 3 – CUT! Again ask Archangel Michael to take it to the light to be restored and healed.

Phase 4: Golden Light

When you've finished with the mirror, locate the centre of the room. There you should find a place to sit comfortably. Take your seat. Just above it, you'll notice a glorious and divine golden light. Please allow this golden light to enter your body both on a physical level and an etheric level. Golden light is the most powerful light. It will cleanse and protect you.

ACCEPTANCE

And it will also put loving energy into an empty place where negative energy formerly was stored. Let it fill up all those gaps where your old habits and old energy was taking up space.

As you sit here, awash in golden light, take three slow, deep breaths in through your nose, and then exhale the air through your mouth. Imagine yourself becoming calmer with each deep inhalation. See yourself releasing the stress of the day with every full exhalation.

Phase 5: Take Away

Scan the room for anything you need to take with you telepathically—such as a flower, a rock, or a crystal. Please take this object and put it in your pocket as a symbol of having made your journey. It is not uncommon to find symbolic objects in physical reality soon after doing a Higher Self Connection Meditation. If you do, take it as a sign of being on the right track.

Now you can head out the door, ensuring as you do that it is once again locked and the room is protected behind you. Walk down the stairs leading back to your beautiful garden.

Once you are in the garden again, it is time to make the trip back to your physical body. Begin by hearing the sounds in the room where you are sitting: sounds of the music, your breath, and traffic in the distance.

Wiggle your toes and fingers, and then, without rushing, when you feel ready . . . open your eyes.

Take a few minutes to write down everything that just happened for your future reference.

Please visit the realms of the higher self often. You'll be amazed to see how the room changes and new information appears. This is an excellent way to receive guidance on coping with current challenges, obstacles, and relationships, and to heal emotional wounds.

I am grateful to Margaret Saunders for inspiring this exercise.

Exercise 2: Cutting the Chains

Cutting emotional cords to people from our past, including those we love on the other side, enables us to release energy that wounds us, while keeping the love. I was honoured to learn the importance of severing these bonds from the beautiful Doreen Virtue in 2011 and created this ritual, which is adapted from her teachings.

Every interaction that we have creates an energetic attachment between us and that person or even object. This happens whether we are aware of it or not. The concept of cutting the chains is all about

ACCEPTANCE

releasing ourselves from any negative energy that may be lingering.

This is not to say that we do not love or care for that person but rather that we want to move on free from any unwanted energy that we have unknowingly been holding onto. It is actually a very loving act to do. It can be done with people who we are still in a relationship with (not just romantic relationship, but any type, including those in a workplace) and it can even be done for someone deceased.

When I think of chains, I think of big metal chains that are connecting us to that person. This is because it is quite a heavy object and that is the energy feeling that we can often have. Think of it this way, if a person is diagnosed with a sexually transmitted disease they are required to inform their past sexual partners, as it is a duty of care. That person is required to share the information and so and so forth. Likewise, the chains that are connecting us and a certain person also contain the energy of other people that they are connected to. It is a comforting concept to feel that we are all connected; but not in this manner. What this kind of connection means is that we may be unknowingly tapping into the energy stream of hundreds of thousands of people, both the good and the bad. In other words, we are impacted by their love and their fear.

IGNITE YOUR JOY

Note: We want to keep the love that exists between us and the person (even if you feel hurt or betrayed, there is still a love that exists spiritually at the very least). Here is what to do to cut the fear-based chains:

1. Go to a place where you will be uninterrupted and feel at peace. You may wish to light a candle or put some soothing music on to set a harmonious ambiance.

2. Make a note, either mentally or on paper, of the people who you would like to release now.

3. Sit comfortably or lie down.

4. Start by taking three deep breaths in through your nose and exhaling the air through your mouth. With every in-breath, imagine breathing in peace and tranquillity. With every out-breath, imagine letting go of stress and tension.

5. Imagine a beautiful egg of light surrounding your physical and energetic body. This can be any colour or colours that you wish. I like to use white, gold, or pink.

6. Next, simply imagine the first person on your list. Notice where the energy chains between you are attached. Are they around your hips, your hands? Where do they link to the other person? What colour are the chains? How big or small are they? You may feel as if you are just making answers up, and that is fine.

ACCEPTANCE

Allow your conscious mind to show you the chains or think whatever it wants to.

7. Once you are clear on the size of the chains and where they are connected to your body, visualise a light the same colour as the egg of light you imagined at the start of this practice. See this light as if it was a Jedi lightsaber from the movie *Star Wars*. Imagine it cutting through the metal chains one by one and melting them away.

8. This process may take a couple of seconds or it may take a few minutes, depending on the depth of the relationship and the amount of fear that existed between you and the other person.

9. Once you have managed to melt the chains, imagine whatever remnants may still be lying on the floor as being transformed into light and sent out into the universe. You have transformed the chains of fear into light and love.

10. Next, check the location where the chains were on both you and the other person. Are there any holes there? If there are, imagine that another light arrives to heal the wounds. Visualise that light filling any gaps or even stitching up the wounds until they entirely disappear.

11. Lastly, place your dominant hand over your heart and feel gratitude toward the person you have disconnected from, even if, or

IGNITE YOUR JOY

especially if, they hurt you. This is an important part of the process. If they really hurt you, this is a time to let go and forgive them. Remember that this is about forgiving and releasing the person and yourself, not necessarily saying you accept the actions that a person took.

12. Repeat steps 6-11 until you feel you have cut the chains of everyone on your list.

When you are done, rest quietly. Take a walk and get some air. Allow your energy system to adjust and become stable. Over the next few days, you may notice you are operating in a lighter way as you move through the world. Something will have shifted, and time will reveal what this is. You should feel less of a drain on your energy and more like your natural soul self.

"It is important to acknowledge and embrace the concept of death, which is a normal and necessary part of life. In Eastern cultures, it is common to have celebrations and activities surrounding death. This is healthy and cleansing.

"Humans are mortal creatures. Life is impermanent. Once you are able to accept and release any fears surrounding death you can let go and live in the moment."

The Mothers' Club

PART IV
YOUR PROFIT IS WAITING

Unless you live in a society where money is no longer required (though you probably wouldn't be reading this book if you were) you will need to understand the often elusive and mysterious entity called money. I see financial freedom as the last piece of the joy puzzle. Hopefully, this section of the book will help you to demystify some of your own confusion about money and the role it plays in the journey of you.

One of the things that fills me with joy is to imagine a time when truly awakened souls—those who want to leave our world a better place than when they entered it—are able to live in financial freedom. So many people share this desire. Of course, money should not be the be all and end all of everything we do; however, if we do not come to a place of understanding in our relationship with money we sacrifice a lot of the joy, love, and purpose that are possible for us.

CHAPTER 10
WHAT DOES MONEY MEAN TO YOU?

"Too many people spend money they haven't earned, to buy things they don't want, to impress people they don't like."

Will Smith

Money is a vehicle for valuable life experiences. It enables us to create wonderful, meaningful experiences for ourselves and others. Feeling abundant has little or nothing to with the amount of money in your bank account or your purse or pocket. It really has to do with the energetic relationship that you have to receiving and managing whatever it is that money represents to you. For example, if money represents security to you, then the real issue you need to contend with in life is finding ways to feel more secure. If money represents love, then the issues are how to be free enough to give and receive love, and to love yourself.

Please note that how you relate to money is not a conscious process. If it was, then you would already have all the money that you desire or require, because how you handle money would be aligned differently than it is now. Clearly this goes a lot deeper than that.

Let's examine, for a moment, two ways many people relate to money. Have a look at these scenarios.

- **Scenario 1:** You have money and you fear losing it.
- **Scenario 2:** You do not have money and your sole focus is on attaining it.

In both of these scenarios, the emotional and energetic experience is exactly the same: Both are fear based. If you were to put yourself into the emotional state of the person in Scenario 1, what types of feelings, experiences, and emotions might you be having? Stress? Exhaustion? Confusion? Anxiety? Living in the past? Concern for the future?

What about in Scenario 2? How might you be feeling and experiencing life? Stress? Exhaustion? Confusion? Anxiety? Living in the past? Concern for the future?

You see, if we have money there can be a tendency to fear losing it. This is what has commonly been referred to as the lottery effect. I have heard it said that those who win the lottery tend to lose all the

WHAT DOES MONEY MEAN TO YOU?

money they won within two years of winning. Why would this be so? If we are all comfortable at a certain level of affluence, could it be that bankruptcy or poverty actually has very little to do with how much money you possess and more to do with your direct relationship with money. In other words, your level of affluence or poverty is in many ways a by-product of how you feel about money on an unconscious level, and what you unconsciously believe it feels about you. Interestingly, we all relate to money as if it is a person or an entity with intelligence and feelings.

Let me ask you a question. If you want more money than you currently possess, why do you want the money? Is it because you believe the money would enable you to buy a "better life," "freedom," "happiness," "joy," "love," "respect," or help you fulfill another specific desire you have? In reality, what money can buy you is experiences. What is not clear is if those experiences will necessarily "buy" you the better life, freedom, happiness, joy, respect, or love, and so on, that you desire.

Well, I guess we don't really know whether or not money can make us happy until we try spending money to be happy. However, if we look at the facts to see what they reveal about people's experiences, we begin to see that money is only a vehicle and that the actual commodity we are exchanging it for is something very different indeed. Clearly we enjoy witnessing and exploring this concept given the success of such movies as *Trading Places* (1983), *The*

IGNITE YOUR JOY

Shawshank Redemption (1994), and *Jerry Maguire* (1996), to name a few.

The standard definition of profit is: "A financial benefit that is realised when the amount of revenue gained from a business activity exceeds the expenses, costs, and taxes needed to sustain the activity."[1] But what does profit mean to you, personally? Although this chapter is about financial gain, it is also about the emotional and spiritual gains we make in our lives. Considering the original definition of profit, can you imagine how this concept could apply to your emotional and spiritual life?

How many times have you found yourself in scenarios where you have not profited? Where the energy you have given out was far greater than what you received in return? In this part of the book, we're talking about how to avoid experiencing uneven or unrewarding situations in the future.

Isn't it time that you profited in every area of your life? Isn't it time that:

- You gained financially?
- Your health improved?
- You developed spiritually?
- You felt content?
- Peace?
- Love?

WHAT DOES MONEY MEAN TO YOU?

Anything you wish to experience is available to you when you choose to accept that it is.

What is money really? To everyone, it means something different. Ask a successful stockbroker this question and you will get a very different answer than the one you get when you ask a person living on a pension. Money is a topic that can inspire a lot of passion and interest. It also can raise a lot of aggression, frustration, and fear.

Money is a screen on which we can project feelings. However, it is really a neutral screen—wouldn't you agree? The purely financial definition of money is as a tool for exchanging products and services, a medium of exchange. I also define money as an opportunity to grow personally, professionally, and spiritually, and as a means for giving back to my world.

How do you define money? Do you have another take on its role in your life?

An interesting fact about money is how it was invented. In his book *The Critical Path*, R. Buckminster Fuller writes: "Up until 1500 B.C., all money was cattle, lambs, goats, or pigs—*live* money that was real life-support wealth, wealth you could actually eat. Steers were by far the biggest food animal and so they were the highest denomination of money. The Phoenicians carried their cattle with them for trading, but these big creatures proved to be very cumbersome on long voyages. This was the time when

IGNITE YOUR JOY

Crete was the headquarters of the big-boat people and their new supreme weapon: the lines-of-supply control ship. . . . The pair of joined bulls horns symbolized that the particular ship carried real-wealth traders—that there were cattle on board to be exchanged for local-wealth items. . .

"Graduating from carrying cattle along for trading in 1500 B.C., the Phoenicians invented metal money, which they first formed into iron half-rings that looked like a pair of bull's horns. (Many today mistake them for bracelets.) Soon the traders found that those in previously unvisited foreign countries had no memory of the cattle-on-board trading days and didn't recognize the miniature iron bull horn. If metal was being used for trading then there were other kinds of metal they preferred trading with people—silver, copper, and gold were easy to judge by hefting and were more aesthetically pleasing than the forged iron bull horn symbols.

"This soon brought metal coinage into the game of world trading with the first coin bearing the image of the sovereign of the homeland of the Phoenicians."[2]

Two things stood out for me as I was researching the history of money:

- The ways in which we earn money.
- The ways in which we spend money.

The physical tool we exchange and know as money

WHAT DOES MONEY MEAN TO YOU?

has gotten smaller and smaller. Nowadays, money also exists in intangible forms, such as numbers on a spreadsheet. In Fuller's book he describes how the Phoenicians had to transport large animals for barter across distances of miles and miles. Compare that to how you can now use a credit card that you can swipe through an electronic device at the checkout counter or a series of numbers you can input on your computer screen or smartphone. Can we agree that spending would seem different to individuals who have to hold their money on their backs than it does to us? Can you see how the emotional associations to money and energetic connections are going to be different for people in these two different scenarios?

If you were living in the first scenario, you would know what you were carrying. You would feel your wealth (or lack thereof) with every single step you took. In the second scenario, which represents the modern lifestyle, we often have a sense of total disconnection from our money by contrast.

Through advancements in technology, we certainly have become able to do some incredible things, such as connecting to practically anyone anywhere in the world. However, technology has come at a price—physical connections, and bonding. We now frequently lack intense human physical and spiritual connections: eye contact, hugs, holding hands, and a feeling of belonging to something greater than yourself. This death of skin-to-skin contact leaves us with a feeling of absence, of missing something essential to our souls and our hearts. Although it enables us to remain in closer contact with loved ones who are far away, communications technology is so addictive that it often interferes with simple human exchanges.

CHAPTER 11
WELCOME CONSCIOUS CASH

"'Making money isn't hard in itself,' he complained. 'What's hard is to earn it doing something worth devoting one's life to.'"

Carlos Ruiz Zafón

Conscious cash is money you earn by engaging in work that speaks to your soul and helps you and others to grow. Not only can doing business authentically and consciously for the betterment of the world help you to increase your financial resources, it also can help you to profit in the form of love, joy, and other things you desire in all areas of your life.

One of the most incredible things about earning money consciously and soulfully is that you will enjoy your work more. When you are joyful, you will automatically make more money! Why? Because if what you're doing to generate revenue is in alignment with your core values and authentic self you will be more effective in your work and you will also be more deliberate in your spending habits.

When we make money doing things that are not authentic to our souls, we tend to:

- Not make enough of it. Instead we avoid working and our efforts are hollow.

- Spend too much of it. Unconsciously we don't feel we deserve to keep what we gained, or we spend to give ourselves pleasure to compensate for hating our jobs.

Doing either of these things means you have adopted a poverty mentality. If you habitually operate in the manner of excessive spending or inadequate earning then you will eventually go broke.

Perhaps you are familiar with the law of attraction: "Like attracts like." Let's play with this idea for a moment. Whether you agree or disagree on the surface of it, by using this definition something interesting about your personal finances may be revealed.

If you hate your job or your business, isn't it likely that you unconsciously hate money and want it to get lost? Energetically, your job and finances are connected. You earned your money through a means that disgusts you, so you are likely to try to get rid of it by spending it on things that you don't really

WELCOME CONSCIOUS CASH

need in order to feel more whole. Perhaps you hope that buying material things can give you a quick hit of positive feeling to compensate for spending so much of your life grinding away at an activity you despise or which does not feed the passion and purpose of your soul.

By contrast, if you are working and living authentically, you probably want to stay close to the energy of your money. You are likely to make purchases that somehow represent investments in yourself. From time to time, you may still go out and buy a pair of shoes or a tailored jacket you impulsively want, but there's a difference between spending out of love and unconscious spending. Now you are buying items that reflect your conscious self.

If you are earning money doing what you love, what stops you from keeping it?

If you are not doing what you love, is it time now to discover a bigger purpose?

You were provided with some guidance on identifying your purpose in Part Three. Go back and review those chapters. If you feel that you require more help, please refer to the Resources section at the back of the book.

Discovering a bigger purpose doesn't require you to quit your job or leave your current business. Not necessarily. It only requires you to actively participate in

IGNITE YOUR JOY

a journey of self-awareness. In order to really benefit from that journey, you will need to accept the following ten statements as truth. If you are unable to accept them right away, that is okay. Please allow yourself time to process them and let them land in your consciousness wherever they need to. When you are ready to examine them more closely you will.

Ten Truths about Abundance

Truth #1. Every single person has access to the same abundance of the universe—in all its forms: Therefore, you have spiritual, emotional, and financial access to abundance.

Truth #2. You are an empowered human being and create experiences for yourself both consciously and unconsciously.

Truth #3. Your past employment history doesn't define you.

Truth #4. Your past financial experiences don't define your future abundance.

Truth #5. The outer abundance you see is a direct reflection of your internal world.

Truth #6. Those around you mirror your abundance or scarcity. The level of abundance you see in the lives of others is what you see in yourself.

Truth #7. Every experience in life is an opportunity for personal growth.

Truth #8. Every person you come in contact with is your teacher.

Truth #9. There is no negative or positive, there only IS.

Truth #10. Like other objects, money is energy. As such, it can be used for good or for bad purposes.

Conscious vs. Unconscious Money Relationships

The ten truths about abundance are so powerful that they have the potential to change your life dramatically. That is, if you are willing to believe them. How can you go about doing that? A great way is to set up a ten-day practice. Begin by simply taking one truth at a time and use it throughout the day for one day. Use it as a daily focus or meditation, much the same way as the book *A Course in Miracles* uses daily practices. So for example, on Day 1 your focus would be to imagine: "Every single person has access to the same abundance of the universe—in all its forms: Therefore, I have spiritual, emotional, and financial access to abundance."

What does believing this do for you?

What do you notice physically, emotionally, or spiritually on Day 1?

How did you interact with people?

Imagination is a great way to begin exploring a new idea, as it is generally something we can do quite easily. If I told you to imagine you were riding a unicorn to your job while reading the paper, you could probably do it. Most people can do that. You may feel silly holding this image in mind, but you can do it. If you can't do it easily, then practice for a while until you build up your imagination muscle.

The way that I understand the process of adopting a new belief is that we must understand it on three levels:

- Intellectually.
- Emotionally.
- Spiritually/energetically.

WELCOME CONSCIOUS CASH

Most of us tend to comprehend new information only intellectually at first. As we take on a concept, we examine it rationally and then place it in any pre-existing mental box that it seems to fit. We compare it to similar and dissimilar theories, and then label it good or bad by contrast to those.

If we deem a particular concept worthy of more time and energy, we then allow ourselves to experience it on an emotional level. What this means is that we play around with new ideas by testing them out in our lives, developing benchmarks to see if they work. If an idea works, the next level is to understand the concept on an energy level. This is the spiritual level known as embodiment. By the time you have mastered a concept and tested it in your life, you breathe it, own it, and do not necessarily even notice it, register it, or particularly care about it. It just is part of who you are and how you function.

So in this instance, what might you feel about the idea: "Every single person has access to the same abundance of the universe—in all its forms: Therefore, I have spiritual, emotional, and financial access to abundance"?

If you feel that you can accept this idea, it becomes part of you energetically. To me, embodiment is about having a knowingness, which is more than a belief. It would be like asking, "Do you believe that the Earth is round?" I do not believe it is, I know it is.

IGNITE YOUR JOY

Knowing that every person has access to the same abundance of the universe in all its forms means I have explored, played around, seen, felt, or heard whatever I needed to in order for me to know that without question.

I love using the example of the Earth being round. There once was a time in our history when it was believed to be flat. All of us have inner sceptics, which are useful parts of us that analyse and research. Remember to allow your inner sceptic to take a break sometimes so that you can go about exploring that indeed the Earth is actually round now these days.

Many people talk. Many people study, examine, intellectualise, and debate. But as we all know, talk is cheap. Very few people ever actually embody the energy of the ideas they talk about. A Persian proverb teaches, "Seek truth in meditation, not in mouldy books. Look in the sky to find the moon, not in the pond."[1]

Imagine your conscious self as being the tip of an iceberg. Your unconscious self is the rest of the iceberg. The unconscious part of you is filled with stories, thoughts, and beliefs that govern you and motivate your choices on a conscious level. The unconscious mind is very deep and powerful. The more of the stored unconscious material that you can bring up to the conscious level to be seen and considered, the more capable you will be of making strong and empowered decisions.

WELCOME CONSCIOUS CASH

Earning vs. Spending

In traditional psychology, the unconscious is considered a reflection of our present-day lives. In conscious cash, it is also understood to include the soul and the journeys the soul has been on for however many thousands of years that it has been in existence. The goal is never to awaken the entirety of the unconscious mind, as that would be an exhausting feat. Instead, the goal is to understand and know ourselves deeply on the levels of our humanity and soul consciousness so that we may be the best version of ourselves.

During university, I studied the ecological systems theory developed by child psychologist Urie Bronfenbrenner, well known for being the creator of the U.S. Head Start Program.[2] Also known as human ecology theory, this construct describes psychological development as occurring within five types of nested environments, with bidirectional influences within and between these systems.

The five systems are:

1. **Microsystem.** Your immediate environments (family, school, workplace, peer group, neighbourhood).

2. **Mesosystem.** The direct connections between the various immediate environments in your world. It contains interactions where two microsystems overlap, such as when your friends attend a family gathering.

3. **Exosystem.** The environments that only indirectly affect you (community, religion, extended family, or the broadcast and print media, for example). It contains settings that you are not actively involved with, which nonetheless have a significant influence on you, such as your spouse's workplace. An example of an impactful event taking place in an exosystem would be if your husband or wife was laid off from his or her job.

4. **Macrosystem.** The larger cultural context in which you live (for example, an Eastern or Western country with its own unique national economy and political culture; or an ethnic or religious subculture).

5. **Chronosystem.** The patterns of environmental events and transitions that you're immersed in over the course of your lifespan. This system consists of all of the experiences that you have had during your existence.

I have added a sixth and seventh system to this model, which are:

6. **The Earth's energy system.** This refers to the energetic personality of our planet over time

and space. Feel (or imagine if you cannot feel it) the state of Mother Earth prior to World War II and afterwards. Feel or imagine the state of Mother Earth prior to 9/11 and post 9/11. Now imagine the state of Mother Earth in 1715 and in 2015. Do you feel or notice a difference? Earth has an energetic footprint, which it has carried for billions of years.

7. **The universe's energy system.** This refers to everything that one could humanly imagine as being vast and universal. We could describe this as including other dimensions, the angelic realm, guided masters, souls in transit, parallel universes, and so on. Just like you live on Mother Earth, you live within the universe.

There are many more levels and systems that could be added to this model, however I fear that our humanity limits us from understanding them just yet.

Now that you have an awareness of these seven environments as systems, imagine for a moment how this framework affects your views on money. Of course, the framework affects how you perceive every concept from love, to education, community, and more. Here, we are mainly examining the concept of money.

Let's break down your views on money now. Take a few minutes now to answer these questions on your own or to discuss them with a friend.

- How do you view money? (Consciously and unconsciously)
- How does (or did) your mum/dad/ siblings view money?
- How do your friends and work colleagues view money?
- How do your acquaintances view money?
- How do the media you read or watch portray money?
- How does your neighbourhood and community view money?
- How does your religion/culture/countrymen view money?
- How have your experiences in your life affected your view of money?
- How does Mother Earth view money?
- How does your higher self-view money?
- How did your dearly departed view money? (Just as far back as you can imagine.) Take into consideration the circumstances under which they lived, such as wars or famines.
- Imagine how the universe views money.

When you can become more and more aware of just how many factors actually contribute to your beliefs and identity as it pertains to money (or anything else

WELCOME CONSCIOUS CASH

for that matter) you can realise just how small and large the ripples money creates within its ocean.

In order to become more conscious, ask yourself these two questions.

- How do I want to view money?

- How do I want my kids, my family, my community, my world, and my universe to view money?

You are a responsible and integral part of each of the aforementioned seven systems.

Isn't it time to recognise that any sense of shortage you might have had, whether you are working on getting out of debt or on earning your first million dollars, is an opportunity for you to transform any sense of "not enough" into the sense of "being abundant"?

Once you ask yourself the two questions above, be prepared for the work that is involved with creating the reality that so many of us are seeking: abundance on all levels.

You may be saying, "Debbie, if it is as easy as you say, then tell me how to create more abundance."

Here you go . . .

CHAPTER 12
PRACTICAL EXERCISES TO CREATE ABUNDANCE

"Abundance and lack are parallel realities; every day I make the choice of which one to inhabit."

Sarah Ban Breathnach

Let's begin with an exercise.

The Benchmark Exercise

In your experience, does money naturally fall into one of these two categories?

- **Sexy (positive):** travel, health support, charity/giving back, positive events.

- **Scary (negative):** loss of identity, loss of friends/support network, loss of "what to do" with my time if I have so much money I don't need to work anymore.

IGNITE YOUR JOY

Some people decide it's not worth the risk of having money, and that they would rather play the poor game than play the rich game.

Playing the rich game exposes you to yourself. For example, you may ask:

- "Do people only like me for my money?"
- "Am I giving enough to charity?"
- "Should I spend money on x or on y?"

You see, money creates freedom, but it also creates choice. Choice in itself can be freeing and sexy, or it can be suffocating and scary. It can create overwhelm and fear of doing the wrong thing; and probably the biggest problem of all, it can create fear of losing it all and having nothing.

This may sound odd, as obviously you want to be experiencing the sexy side of money. However, wanting something is simply not enough. If you have beliefs and experiences that are scary, on some level this means you are afraid to actually have whatever it is that you say you want. As a way to stay safe, you may be unconsciously creating ways to avoid having money. This phenomenon is also known as self-sabotage.

This exercise is simply about noticing when you find yourself in a place of fear rather than love. So in this instance, fear is scary money and love is sexy money. This exercise is not about judging yourself or any-

PRACTICAL EXERCISE TO CREATE ABUNDANCE

one else. It is about becoming aware of what you're thinking and feeling so that you have the opportunity to transform negative patterns.

Here is how you can identify which one you may be focusing on at any given moment. Become acutely aware of your thoughts, feelings, and actions. These are interconnected. Ask yourself:

- What am I thinking?
- What am I feeling?
- How am I acting?

If you can see that any or all your thoughts, feelings, and actions are negative, then move on to any of the following exercises to bring you from fear to love. As Marianne Williamson repeatedly asserts in her book *A Return to Love,* a miracle is "a shift in perception" from fear to love.[1]

The Beliefs Exercise

In Chapter 11, we discussed exploring and playing around with new ideas and beliefs as a way to find out what works best in your life. This exercise asks you to look at your current beliefs—especially the ones that seem negative to you—and then substitute an alternate, more positive belief that you can play around with. Do this to see what shows up in your world as a result of this newfound belief.

Below are some examples of how this works.

- **Current belief:** Earning money is easy, keeping it is hard.

- **New belief:** Earning and saving money is effortless.

- **Current belief:** Having money means I am responsible for everyone's happiness.

- **New belief:** Having money means I can choose to help when it feels right for me.

- **Current belief:** My friends will hate me, be jealous of me or use me.

- **New belief:** My friends will be inspired and happy for me.

- **Current belief:** Having that kind of freedom/lifestyle will be boring, what will I do with my life?

- **New belief:** Having money means the world is my oyster and I can choose from so many wonderful things to do.

Cognitive Behavioural Therapy (CBT) for Old Beliefs

Just in case you are human, and therefore do not know how to switch from an old to a new belief in the blink of an eye, here is a great three-step exercise

PRACTICAL EXERCISE TO CREATE ABUNDANCE

for you. Start with any belief you'd like to change. For example: I am really bad with money.

Step 1. Ask yourself: What evidence do I have to suggest that this thought is true? You may find evidence that suggests you are bad with money. Sometimes you may have physically lost money or you might not know how much you earn.

Step 2. Ask yourself: What evidence do I have that suggests that this thought is untrue? You may find evidence that you are good with money, such as that you always have had a well-paying job. Perception is the key here. So let's say that you have some evidence for both.

Step 3. Ask yourself: Is holding this belief serving me positively? If it is not, then it is actually as simple as changing that thought to a positive and believable one, such as I am learning to be good with money. Notice that the word learning is acceptable to your mind. Once you change the original thought to a more positive one, you can also change your feelings and actions.

Remember to accept whatever feelings and thoughts arise during the exercise. And, oh yeah, also remember to breathe.

Integrating Your New Beliefs Exercise

Integration is a process, so allow yourself some time to adjust to any newfound knowledge and awareness. I find it helpful to know that this process of integration, like much of life, comes in cycles. Just as soon as you have acquired wisdom, you will more than likely be questioning another concept or belief. I liken this phenomenon to cleaning the dishes. When I first moved out of my family home, where I was incredibly lazy and thought that the dishes cleaned themselves (my mum did them), it took me a good few years to get use to the process that the dishes would constantly be in some phase of the cycle of clean and dirty. They would either be stowed away, which meant that—yay! —I was free, or they would be clean and needing to be put away, or they would be dirty and needing to be washed. I would become anxious every time they were not in the first stage. Then one day, I realised, This is how it is unless I hire a full-time maid, so I had better just learn to be okay with whatever phase of clean the dishes are in.

It is the same for growth. It is what it is. No phase is better than any other, although some phases are more unpleasant or uncomfortable. But so what?

I realised (after I tested it), that I felt so much better about the dishes and life in general when I held the belief, "It is what it is."

PRACTICAL EXERCISE TO CREATE ABUNDANCE

Here are the phases that you may go through in order to integrate a new belief.

- **Belief:** This is when you begin to notice a belief that is not very helpful or worse; it is actually making you feel bad (just like my dishes experience). This is a time where you may look at coming up with a new, more beneficial belief.

- **Feelings/emotions:** This is when you begin to notice if the new belief is actually giving you a better more fulfilling and positive experience of life.

- **Action:** This is testing the waters in the real world. Just thinking or believing is not enough. You must step out of your head and interact with people during different circumstances in your life. Let's say, as an example, that you have moved away from the belief "I am lousy with money" to "I am learning to be good with money." What actions have you taken or might you take that would support the belief that you are indeed "learning to be good with money"? An example might be:

    > Hiring a good accountant.

    > Reading a book about budgeting.

    > Actually looking at what you have in the bank.

    > Writing down a list of income and expenses.

- **Practice:** Like all good things, putting beliefs into action requires practice. You must practice, practice, practice, until this new belief becomes a habitual part of your everyday life. You may find in the beginning that you want to go back to believing the old belief, not because it is better for you, but simply because it is so ingrained in you and has been part of your life for so many years that you have been you. When this happens move on to the next step of integration: acceptance.

- **Acceptance:** In the moment when an old belief emerges, notice it and say to yourself, "Oh hey, you old familiar belief! Yeah, thanks for popping in." That is it. That is all you have to do. Simply by noticing it, you will naturally shift back to the focus of the new belief.

**Shifting Your Energetic Focus Exercise
(aka the Door)**

This is a simple exercise that my incredible business mentor, Mihir Thaker, taught me. It is something that I do and recommend my clients do throughout the day.

Start by taking a few deep breaths and going within. Imagine two doors in front of you. One represents fear (or scary money, in this instance), while the other represents love (or sexy money). For me, the fear door is always on the left and the love door on the

PRACTICAL EXERCISE TO CREATE ABUNDANCE

right. I encourage you to picture them in the same way, as generally the left represents the past, and the right the future.

Just take a moment and notice: Where is your energy facing? Is it facing the left door or the right door? Without any judgment, just notice. Then, in your mind's eye, make the shift so that you are energetically focusing where you want to go.

Recognising the Job Your Unconscious Parts Are Doing

One of the most profound experiences I had came when I attended a workshop called Money Magic, which was by a remarkable coach named Michelle Masters. She assisted the group so beautifully to connect to unconscious parts of our minds that were unknowingly holding us back from attracting more money. The essence of her teaching was to acknowledge that many of those parts had been employed by a younger version of ourselves (generally before the age of four) in order to bring us an experience, such as security or happiness.

Assuming that these hidden parts had feelings and an intelligent mind, what they did not know was that they were holding us back from providing the experience they'd been created to provide. This may have been for a number of reasons, but generally it was because when we hired them to keep us safe (or another reason) we were two or three. Now, at age thirty or forty or fifty, we had outgrown them.

Michelle guided us to thank these parts for their commitment to us, almost as if they were beloved members of our families, and then lovingly had us explain to them that we had grown and needed a different kind of support.

When I did this exercise, many of my parts felt abandoned. I was instructed by Michelle to offer them another job. She then said, "Check in. Are they happy now?"

I checked in with those parts of me and saw happy faces. If I had left them unhappy, they would likely make themselves known and possibly become destructive (much like a young child trying to get attention).

In order to do this type of work, you generally need to be guided by a highly skilled professional.

In the meantime, a great and simple way that you can get to know what some of your unconscious parts are up to.

- Write down fifty answers to the question: What will I lose by being rich?
- Write down fifty answers to the question: What will I gain by being rich?

PRACTICAL EXERCISE TO CREATE ABUNDANCE

Make Your Purpose Bigger Than Your Fear!

You may be familiar with the idea of your big "why." This is the answer to questions like:

- Why are you involved with a certain project?
- Why are you setting up that business?

These are very important types of questions to ask, for a number of reasons. First, they can help you achieve clarity on who you are serving and what you are hoping to achieve. Second, they will also come in handy when you come up against obstacles.

Have you ever noticed that sometimes when you commit to something, the universe throws you a curve ball? Or many curve balls! If you are clear as to why you are doing that thing, then it will inspire and motivate you when the curve balls are flying toward your bat. You'll be able to keep swinging—and maybe even hit a homerun.

One of my big "whys" is to assist those around me to use financial abundance as a tool to grow their love and purpose even bigger. My goal is to support you to leave your legacy to your family, to charities, and by travelling the world and experiencing other cultures. I am excited to help you create tools such as books, programs, movies, courses, businesses, restaurants, health centres, retreats, and so on, that express your love and purpose.

IGNITE YOUR JOY

Can you imagine a world where more people lived with more love in their hearts? Had more days filled with purpose? That's the world I want to create! That's the legacy I want to leave behind. That vision, that love, that passion so far has outweighed every fear.

I invite you to discover and ignite your joy so that you may create and experience more joy in every facet of your life. I would love to hear about your journey so that together we may spread even more joy.

ACKNOWLEDGMENTS

The first person that must be acknowledged is you, the reader. Thank you for taking the time to be a part of the journey.

Stephanie Gunning, my amazing editor. This book would simply not exist without you. Thank you for always having my back and believing in me.

Ben, my darling husband, thank you for your constant love and unwavering support.

Jonah, thank you for being the beautiful little man that you are. Mummy loves you so much.

Mum and Nanna, although physically not on Earth, you still miraculously supported this writing process from above. I am forever grateful for your unconditional love on Earth and above.

Dad, thank you for your enthusiasm, love, and spiritual guidance always.

Darren, Leah, Ziggy, and Goldie, thank you for your love and pride in me.

Susie, Geoff, Lisa, David, Kim, Ilana, Ros, and Mark, thank you for your love and support.

I would also like to extend my appreciation to the following people:

Eddy, Danny, Bar, and Rik, my amazingly supportive in-laws.

Carly, for over three decades of love and laughter.

Ghania, my soul sister, for the bond we will always share and for inspiring much of what I do.

Mirella, my beautiful teacher and friend.

Mihir, gratitude and love to you for always believing in me.

Benny, Alana, Jacqui, Abby, Tamara, Katherine (Kat), Georgie, Roee, Kaiisha, Lori, and Lachie.

To Fletcher Henry, for his beautiful design of the book and cover; the team at Lincoln Square Books for their efficient production management, copy editing, and counsel and; Jenine Klarenaar from Mecca Creative Marketing and PR.

To all my extended family, friends, and clients, and to the practitioners who have helped me along the way, thank you always.

NOTES

Chapter 1   Why Choose Joy?

Epigraph. Osho, *Joy: The Happiness That Comes from Within* (New York: St. Martin's Griffin, 2009): p. viii.

Chapter 2   Getting Clear on What Brings You Joy

Epigraph. Kay Warren, *Choose Joy: Because Happiness Isn't Enough* (Ada, MI.: Revell, 2012): p. 25.

1. J.D. Salinger, "De Daumier-Smith's Blue Period," *World Review*, vol. 39 (May 1952): pp. 33–48.

2. These words are widely attributed to Winston Churchill, but it is unclear if he actually said or wrote them.

Chapter 3   My Joy Story

Epigraph. Wayne W. Dyer, *Manifest Your Destiny* (New York: HarperCollins Publishers, 1997): p. 76.

Chapter 4   Choose Love Over Fear

Epigraph. John Lennon: https://www.goodreads.com/author/quotes/19968.John_Lennon.

Chapter 5   Be okay with Pissing People Off

Epigraph. This remark was channeled during a conversation I had with members of the Mothers Club in 2013.

Chapter 6   Be Your Own Best Friend

Epigraph. Miguel de Cervantes (1547-1616) was a Spanish novelist, playwright, and poet, best known for his novel *Don Quixote*.

1. Australian Bureau of Statistics. Available at: http://www.abs.gov.au.

2. Statista. Available at: http://www.statista.com/topics/1008/cosmetics-industry.

3. Cosmetic, Toiletry & Perfumery Association. Available at: http://www.ctpa.org.uk.

Chapter 7   Transparent Sisterhood.

Epigraph. This remark was channeled during a conversation I had with members of the Mothers Club in 2013.

1. Mark Twain, *Following the Equator: A Journey Around the World,* vol. 1 (1897).

2. *Marianne Williamson. A Return to Love: Reflections on the Principles of 'A Course in Miracles'* (New York: HarperCollins Publisher, 1992): pp. 190–191.

Chapter 8   Sing Your Song

Epigraph. Michael Limnios, "Dr. Maya Angelou: A Muse in Our Midst," Blues @ Greece (posted June 1, 2013). Available at: http://blues.gr/profiles/blogs/interview-with-dr-maya-angelou-a-muse-who-captivates-audiences.

Chapter 9   Acceptance

Epigraph. Susan Santucci, *Converging Paths: Lessons of Compassion, Tolerance, and Understanding from the East and West* (Boston, MA.: Tuttle Publishing, 2003): p. 81.

1. Belief.net: http://www.beliefnet.com/Quotes/Inspiration/C/Carl-Bard/Though-No-One-Can-Go-Back-And-Make-A-Brand-New-Sta.aspx.

2. *Shirley Valentine*, screenplay by Willy Russell, adapted from the play by Willy Russell, and directed by Lewis Gilbert (1989).

Chapter 10   What Does Money Mean to You?

Epigraph. Will Smith. Available at: http://www.goodreads.com/quotes/322738-too-many-people-spend-money-they-haven-t-earned-to-buy.

1. Profit definition. Available at: http://www.buylocalfood.org/financial-management-101-financial-statements.

2. R. Buckminster Fuller. *The Critical Path* (New York: St. Martin's Press, 1981): pp. 73–75.

Chapter 11   Welcome Conscious Cash

Epigraph. Carlos Ruiz Zafón, *The Shadow of the Wind*, translated by Lucia Graves (New York: Penguin Press, 2004): p. 371.

1. Persian Proverb, cited in Paramahansa Yogananda, *Autobiography of a Yogi* (Los Angeles, CA.: Self-Realization Fellowship, 1998): p. 362.

2. Urie Bronfenbrenner. *The Ecology of Human Development: Experiments by Nature and Design* (Cambridge, MA: Harvard UP, 1979).

1. Chapter 12 Practical Exercises to Create Abundance

Epigraph. Sarah Ban Breathnach, *Simple Abundance: A Daybook of Comfort and Joy* (New York: Warner Books, 1995): foreword.

1. Marianne Williamson. *A Return to Love: Reflections on the Principles of 'A Course in Miracles'* (New York: HarperCollins Publisher, 1992): p. 9.

NEXT STEP

Please head over to IgniteYourJoy.com to register for "Ignite Your Joy: The Online Video Program for Spiritually Minded Entrepreneurs."

Please visit Debbie's website DebbieZita.com to download your free copy of her popular ebook *Nine Lessons about Self-Love Every Woman Should Know* and to find out about her workshops and coaching.

RECOMMENDED RESOURCES

Books on Spiritual Growth

Autobiography of a Yogi by Paramahansa Yogananda

Secrets about Life Every Woman Should Know by Barbara De Angeles

You Can Heal Your Life by Louise Hay

You Can Create an Exceptional Life by Louise Hay and Cheryl Richardson

Healing with the Angels by Doreen Virtue

Crossing Over by John Edward

Am I Going Mad? by Marlyse Carroll

Manifest your Destiny by Dr Wayne Dyer

Living Deliberately by Harry Palmer

91 Days of Q: Questions to Help You Create the Life You Desire by Mary-Anne Liddicoat

The Possibility of Everything by Hope Edelman

A Course in Miracles by Foundation for Inner Peace

Joy: The Happiness That Comes from Within by Osho

Talking to Heaven: A Medium's Message of Life after Death by James Van Praagh

Tuesdays with Morrie: An Old Man, a Young Man, and Life's Greatest Lesson by Mitch Albom

The Alchemist by Paulo Coelho

Veronica Decides to Die by Paulo Coelho

By the River Piedra I Sat Down and Wept by Paulo Coelho

The Way of the Peaceful Warrior by Dan Millman

The Celestine Prophecy by James Redfield

In the Meantime by Iyanla Vanzant

Healing with the Angels by Doreen Virtue

Books on Business/Personal Finances

Millionaire Motivators: How to Find What You Love to Do and Get Paid to Do It by Fiona Jones and Michael R. Dean

Wealthier Than You Think by Paul Squires

The Secrets of My Success—and the Story of Boost Juice—Juice Bits and All by Janine Allis

The E-Myth Revisited: Why Most Small Businesses Don't Work and What to Do about It by Michael E. Gerber

E-Myth Mastery: The Seven Essential Disciplines for Building a World-Class Company by Michael E. Gerber

Books on Parenting

Motherless Mothers: How Mother Loss Shapes the Parents You Become by Hope Edelman

Oracle Card Decks

Healing with the Fairies Oracle Cards by Doreen Virtue

Messages from Your Angels by Doreen Virtue

Goddess Guidance Oracle Cards by Doreen Virtue

Magical Unicorns Oracle Cards by Doreen Virtue

Life Purpose Oracle Cards by Doreen Virtue

The Romance Angels Oracle Cards by Doreen Virtue

Power Thought Cards by Louise Hay

People and Organisations

Abraham-Hicks
www.abraham-hicks.com

Barbara DeAngelis
www.barbaradeangelis.com

Batia and Michelle Grinblat, Founders of Inner Enlightenment Pty. Ltd.
www.innerenlightenmentptyltd.com

Belinda Buchanon, Founder of Hope Child Africa
www.hopechildafrica.org.au

Botanical Medicines
www.botanicamedicines.com.au

Cheryl Richardson
www.cherylrichardson.com

Danielle Roker Tooley, Access Consciousness Facilitator, Kinesiologist, Massage Therapist
www.vitalityandyou.com

Daniel Parmeggiani, International Best Selling Author
www.danielparmeggiani.com

Doreen Virtue
www.angeltherapy.com

Elise Grauer
www.bodhiwellness.com.au

Filiz Halil
www.infiniteu.com.au

Fiona Edelstein, Yoga Instructor, Healer, and Founder of Flavours of Yoga
www.flavoursofyoga.com

Fletcher Henry, Graphic Designer
www.fletchercreative.com

Gabby Bernstein
www.gabbyb.tv

Genine Howard, Editor
www.contentmagazine.com.au

Ghania Dibb, Lawyer and Author
www.diblaw.com.au

Hope Edelman, New York Times Best Selling Author
www.hopeedelman.com
Iyana Vanzant
www.iyanlavanzant.com

Jacqui Christie, Psychologist and Founder of EmPower Me
www.empower-me.com.au

Judy Taylor, Author
www.positivesigns.com.au

Justine McInerney, Singer and Songwriter
www.whoisjmac.com

Kaiisha Taylor, Shaman
www.thehealingtipi.com

Lawrence Ellyard, CEO of IICT
www.iict.com.au

Lisa Cutler
www.cutlercoaching.com

Lori Banks, Spiritual Artist
www.illuminatedspiritart.com.au

Luanne Simmons, Chief Goddess, Global Goddess Gatherer, and Divine Business Mentor of Goddess on Purpose
www.goddessonpurpose.com

Margaret Saunders, Harmonising Energy Coach
www.HarmonisingEnergyCoaching.com
Marianne Williamson
www.mariannewilliamson.com

Mihir Thaker, Executive and Business Coach
www.mihirthaker.com.au

Orsi Parkanyi
www.womenasentrepreneurs.com.au

Osho Foundation
www.osho.com

Padmacahaya International Institute for Inner Study
www.padmacahaya.com

PANDA (Post and Antenatal Depression Association)
www.panda.org.au

Roee Kohn
www.roeekohn.com

Sharon Tal, Founder of Melbourne Kinesiology and Detox Centre
www.mkndc.com.au

Sharyn Matthews
www.Melbournehealthandwellbeing.com

Sophie Trpcevski
www.thegoalspotforwomen.com

Stephanie Gunning, Founding Partner, Lincoln Square Books
www.lincolnsquarebooks.com

Su Jardine
www.alwaysfollowyourheart.com.au

Susan Lily
www.worldpeacefull.com

The Art of Feminine Presence
www.theartoffemininepresence.com

The Festival of the Open Heart
www.padmacahaya.org.au

Toni Reilly, Past Life Therapist, Intuitive Practitioner, and Founder of the Toni Reilly Institute
www.tonireilly.com.au

Your Mantra
www.yourmantraonline.com

Yogananda
www.yogananda-srf.org

ABOUT THE AUTHOR

Debbie Zita is a highly sought-after mentor for women. Her mission in life is to empower one million women to be authentically sexy and successful. Meaning that they feel sexy and confident in their own bodies, have clarity of purpose, and are capable of lovingly creating the financial freedom they deserve.

Debbie has a professional background in the fields of psychology, social work, corporate training, and image consultancy. She holds a bachelor's degree in behavioural science psychology from La Trobe University in Melbourne, a bachelor's degree in social work from Monash University in Melbourne, certificate level 4 in training and assessment from Corporate Training Australia, and a certificate in professional styling from Australian College of Professional Styling. She is also a Doreen Virtue certified angel intuitive® and a member of the International Institute for Complementary Therapists.

Debbie was raised in Melbourne, Australia, in the 1980s in a loving, middle class Jewish family. At university she earned a degree in psychology and social work, but never felt as if she fitted in. From a young age, Debbie could connect with spirits and intuitively knew what people were feeling. She hid this side of her experience until her mother's death in 2008. Her loss left such a deep void in her life that when she began asking herself why she realised that her purpose in life was to help others bridge the gap between the physical world and the spiritual world. Since then, Debbie has been busy changing lives on and off stage at various women's business and spiritual events.

Debbie resides in Melbourne with her son and her husband.

Contact Debbie at DebbieZita.com.

www.ingramcontent.com/pod-product-compliance
Lightning Source LLC
Chambersburg PA
CBHW071906290426
44110CB00013B/1298